The SherThukPens of Arunachal Pradesh

A Narrative of Cultural Heritage and Folklore

The SherThukPens of Arunachal Pradesh

A Narrative of Cultural Heritage and Folklore

by

Anita Sharma

INTACH

Aryan Books International

THE SHERTHUKPENS OF ARUNACHAL PRADESH
A Narrative of Cultural Heritage and Folklore

Text & Photography: Anita Sharma
Natural Heritage Division, INTACH

ISBN: 978-81-7305-444-0

Published in **2013** by
INTACH
The Indian National Trust for Art and Cultural Heritage
71, Lodhi Estate, New Delhi - 110003
and
Aryan Books International
Pooja Apartments, 4B, Ansari Road, New Delhi-110 002 (India)
Tel.: 23287589, 23255799; Fax: 91-11-23270385
E-mail: aryanbooks@gmail.com
www.aryanbooks.co.in

Computer Typeset and Printed in India at
ABI Prints & Publishing Co., New Delhi

Foreword

Tribal societies, located in the frontier regions, have not received adequate attention from scholars, perhaps due to their inaccessibility. The relatively few studies, although rich in material, are dated, having been undertaken much earlier. With growing accessibility, the traditional mores, social organisation and traditional knowledge are fading away before the relentless advance of mainstream civilisation. Much, however, remains to be documented.

The Natural Heritage Division of INTACH has tried to address the knowledge gap and document the culture and social life of these tribes from an anthropological perspective by referring to the earlier studies and supplementing the same with fieldwork. The work has been ably carried out by the author, Ms. Anita Sharma, whose arduous efforts in the field and dedicated research have resulted in this serious contribution to the subject.

The work was supported by a modest grant from the Ministry of Culture, Government of India, during 2004-05. Rather than let the document crumble on some dusty shelf, it was thought appropriate to put the material into the public domain.

Manu Bhatnagar
Principal Advisor
Natural Heritage Division, INTACH

Preface

At the north-eastern tip of India lies the rolling terrain of Arunachal Pradesh, home to snowbound passes, lush forests and deep mysterious valleys. Bounded by Bhutan to the west, Tibet to the north and Burma to the east, the people of Arunachal Pradesh, lived for long, beyond the pale of urbanisation, self-sufficient and proud in their seclusion. They lived as hunters and gatherers. Tribal life in the region, for centuries, whirled around slash-and-burn farming without any significant shift in their internal socio-economic or political structures. External contact was limited and left little lasting impression on their indigenous life. Their culture was a safe repository of the past, which was stored in the collective consciousness of the larger community. However, with the onslaught of modernity, their lives have transformed considerably. Cultures, after all, are invented and defined by their members over time. New dynamics are added and the old are left behind and forgotten. The shift from nomadic to sedentary cultures leads to an evolution of new traditions, mores and material cultures. This, however, does not imply that the prior traditions have been obliterated. Cultures have their own method of continuity and transition. Large tracts of Arunachal yet remain isolated from the city lights and are guardians of traditions, otherwise lost in urban living. The life and culture of remote and rural communities, often characterised by having distinctive customs regarding birth, marriage and death, a moral code, folklore and myths, peculiarities of religious beliefs and rituals, still survive in their rural and urban societies through oral tradition.

The Sherthukpens, a mild-mannered and courteous people, inhabit the region in and around Rupa in the West Kameng district of Arunachal Pradesh. Rupa, the mother village of the Sherthukpens, is at a distance of 19 km from the district headquarters at Bomdila. The main Sherthukpen belt extends westwards from Rupa through a beautiful mountainous gorge, generously sprinkled with rhododendrons, towards Shergaon.

Few scholars and travellers have attempted to map the Sherthukpens in detail. Most studies conducted in the area have only mentioned the Sherthukpens in passing, and almost always clubbed them with the Monpas, their more populous neighbours with whom they share a marked cultural affinity. A monographic study on the Sherthukpens was first attempted by R.R.P. Sharma in 1961, and the Census of India undertook a socio-economic survey of Rupa in 1971. Niranjan Sarkar attempted to analyse and document Buddhism among the Monpas and Sherthukpens in 1980.

The Sherthukpen belt, characterised by its high mountain hamlets, where precarious wooden houses cling to wind-swept hill spines, unravels a richness of diversity and cultural life. This existence is now in direct contact with the mainstream. Roads now have built bridges that were earlier inconceivable. People are fast merging and mingling with the outside world. Isolation and ignorance of the 'other' is being exchanged for awareness and information.

This report has been carried out for the purpose of recording the Sherthukpen society in transition under modern influences. Working under several constraints, the author has managed to explore and gather significant study material and update on the Sherthukpen life. The report's main value lies in analysing the impact of modernity upon their traditional society and the likely loss and evolution of indigenous knowledge and socio-cultural patterns. This study is an endeavour to bring to the fore their vibrant culture, which exhibits its own energy and vigour, their intricate and rich imaginative faculties, and their emotional and ethical states.

The fieldwork for this report was conducted from January to March 2004, and the service of interpreters was often employed for the purpose of research. The primary sources of data were the Sherthukpens of Rupa, Shergaon, Thungri, Gorwa and Doimara. Information was chiefly obtained by observations and interviews, and from secondary sources in the Nehru Memorial Library, New Delhi, and the district library at Bomdila. This study would not have been possible without the relentless patience and generosity extended by all the Sherthukpens encountered in Arunachal Pradesh. Laam Dema's unencumbered friendship opened the first doors for me in Rupa. Mr. Nima Thongchi's family was a source of constant support and encouragement and Dema's magical smile and hospitality worked as a balm after difficult journeys. This study owes a huge debt to Karma Khrimey, Pema Wangdi and Chandu for their humour, insights and companionship, to Netan Dorje Thongon for his thoughtfulness and guidance, and to Pema Chom and his family for their gentleness and strength, so characteristic of the Sherthukpens.

Anita Sharma

DISTRICT MAP OF ARUNACHAL PRADESH

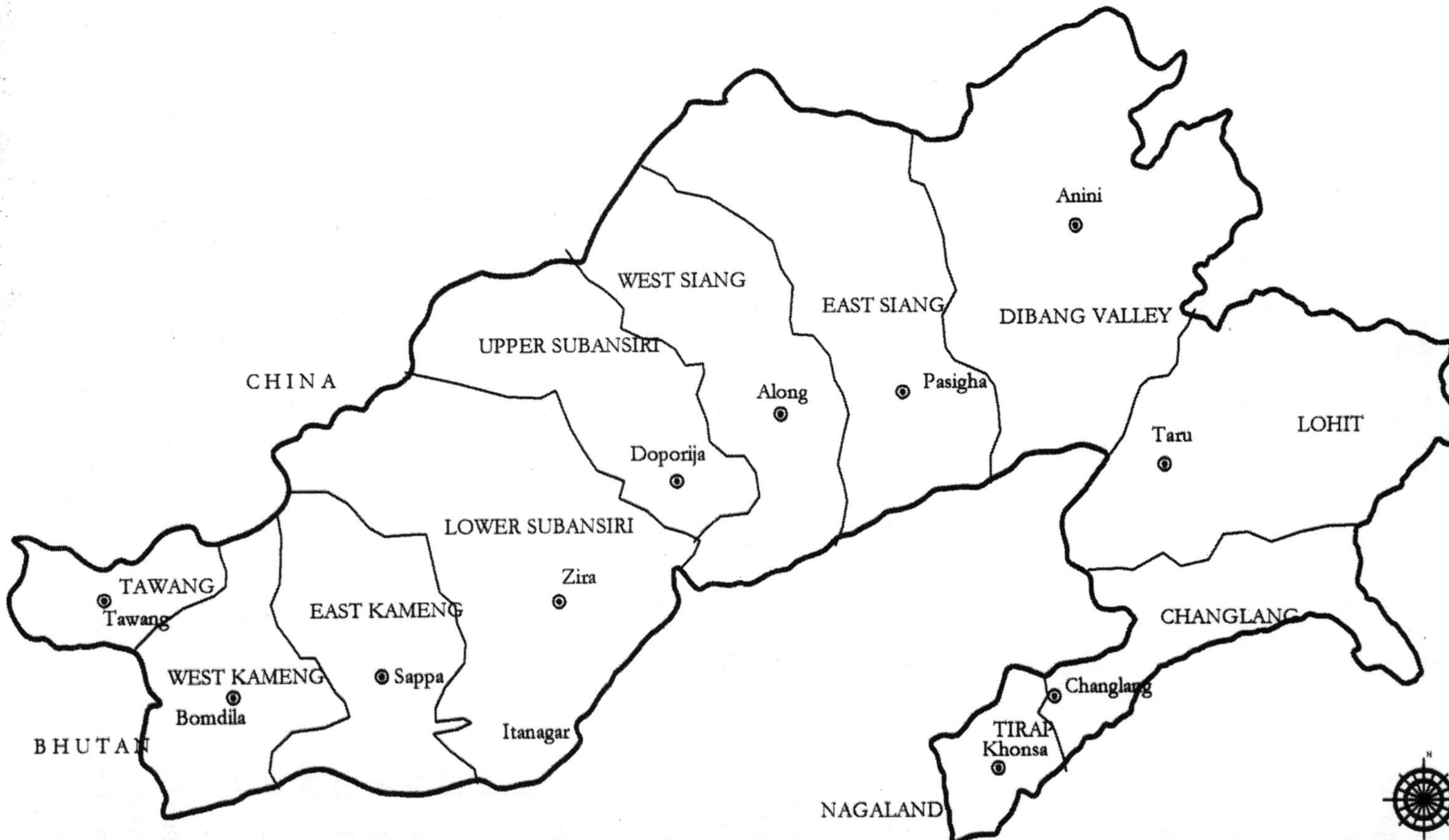

Contents

PHYSIOGRAPHY OF WEST KAMENG REGION

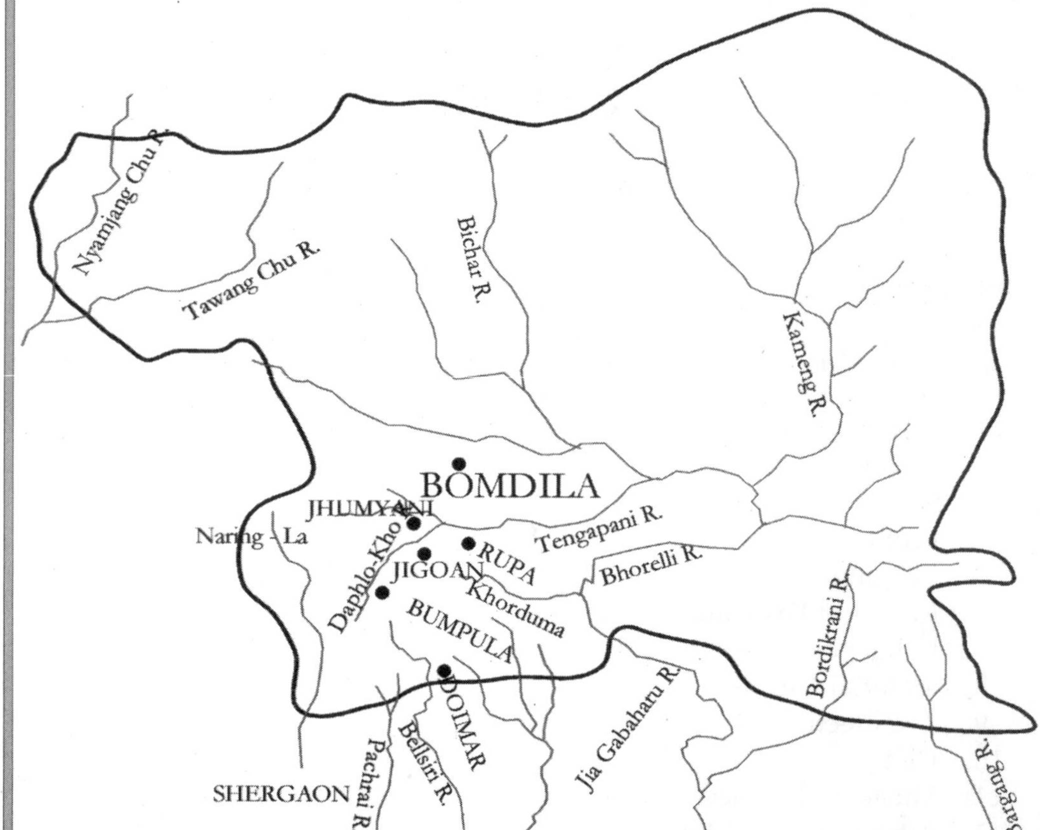

List of Illustrations

Fig. 1. Evening time at Shergaon.

Fig. 2. An old man in Gorwa.

Fig. 3. A Lamaist inscription near the winter camp at Doimara in the foothills.

Fig. 4. Children of Sherthukpens in traditional dress.

Fig. 5. Chaos woman.

Fig. 6. A group of young girls.

Fig. 7. A newly married couple.

Fig. 8. Picture of a typical family.

Fig. 9. Sons traditionally inherit land from the father.

Fig. 14. A woman selling savouries at the weekly foothill bazaar close to Doimara.

Fig. 15. The Sherthukpens were among the first people in the state to use the plough.

Fig. 8. Picture of a typical family.

Fig. 9. Sons traditionally inherit land from the father.

Fig. 10. The Gaonburah of village Thungri.

Fig. 11. Collaborative work being performed by the people of Doimara.

Fig. 12. The people of Thungri performing *gompa* repairs.

Fig. 13. Children playing.

Fig. 14. A woman selling savouries at the weekly foothill bazaar close to Doimara.

Fig. 15. The Sherthukpens were among the first people in the state to use the plough.

Fig. 16. The Sherthukpens traditionally obtained their brass and copper dishes from the Bodo Kacharis.

Fig. 17. A child stands before a Lamaist painting in the Chillipam Monastery.

Fig. 18. Sherthukpens rest outside the Rupa Monastery.

Fig. 19. Tablets inscribed with the mantra *Om mani padme hum* on a *maney*.

Fig. 20. The small gompa at Chillipam.

Fig. 21. Prayer wheels.

Fig. 22. This tree is a Lo spirit of the Sherthukpens.

Fig. 23. *Dzizi* Tshering Norbu Dingla of Rupa is the senior most Lo priest in the Sherthukpen belt.

Fig. 24. The Kamcha or the Lo temple at Rupa.

Fig. 25. A container of water with floating *nampling* petals.

Fig. 26. Sherthukpen women of village Thungri turning the meditative time-wheel.

Fig. 27. A *stupa* constructed by a Sherthukpen in memory of his late mother.

Fig. 28. A young Sherthukpen.

Fig. 29. Medicine man Namgay Sinchaji.

Fig. 30. Sherthukpens have a rich repository of folklore.

Fig. 31. An old lady with oil extracted through indigenous methods.

Fig. 32. Hanganiya herb is commonly used for fractures.

Fig. 33. Weaving is mainly a woman's task.

Fig. 34. A bamboo fish trap.

Fig. 35. A typical textile woven from cotton thread.

Fig. 36. A Bhutanese craftsman working at the Chillipam monastery.

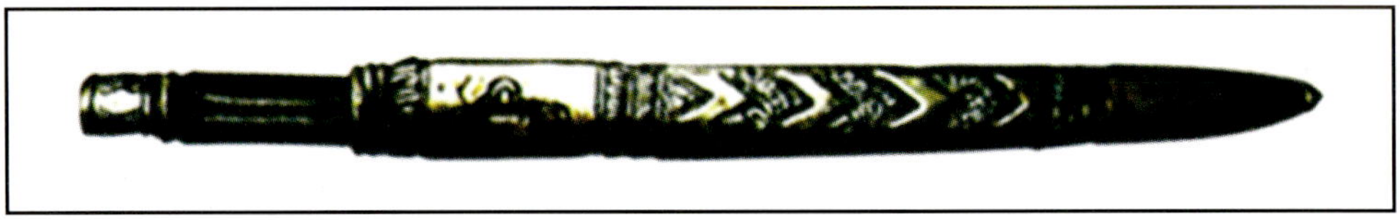

Fig. 37. Sherthukpens of Jigaon are known for their smithy skills.

Fig. 38. A common jewellery item worn by both men and women.

Fig. 39. A Sherthukpen house of bamboo-matting and wood.

Fig. 40. Monastery art in the Rupa Gompa.

Fig. 41. The wooden phallus symbol.

Fig. 42. A Sherthukpen stone house fitted with a window.

Fig. 43. A red chilli chutney or *mircha* is greatly savoured by the Sherthukpens.

Fig. 44. Jabrang is a local herb widely used in cooking, and was employed in trade and barter practices.

Fig. 45. Music and dance comprise the most important recreational activities of the Sherthukpens.

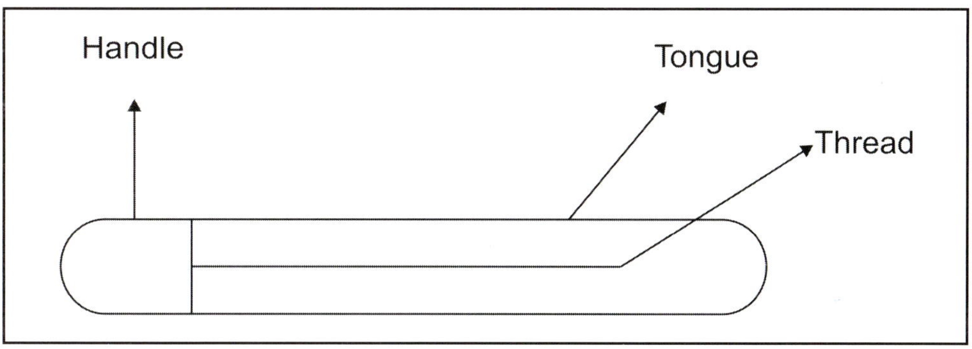

Fig. 46. Bamboo flute.

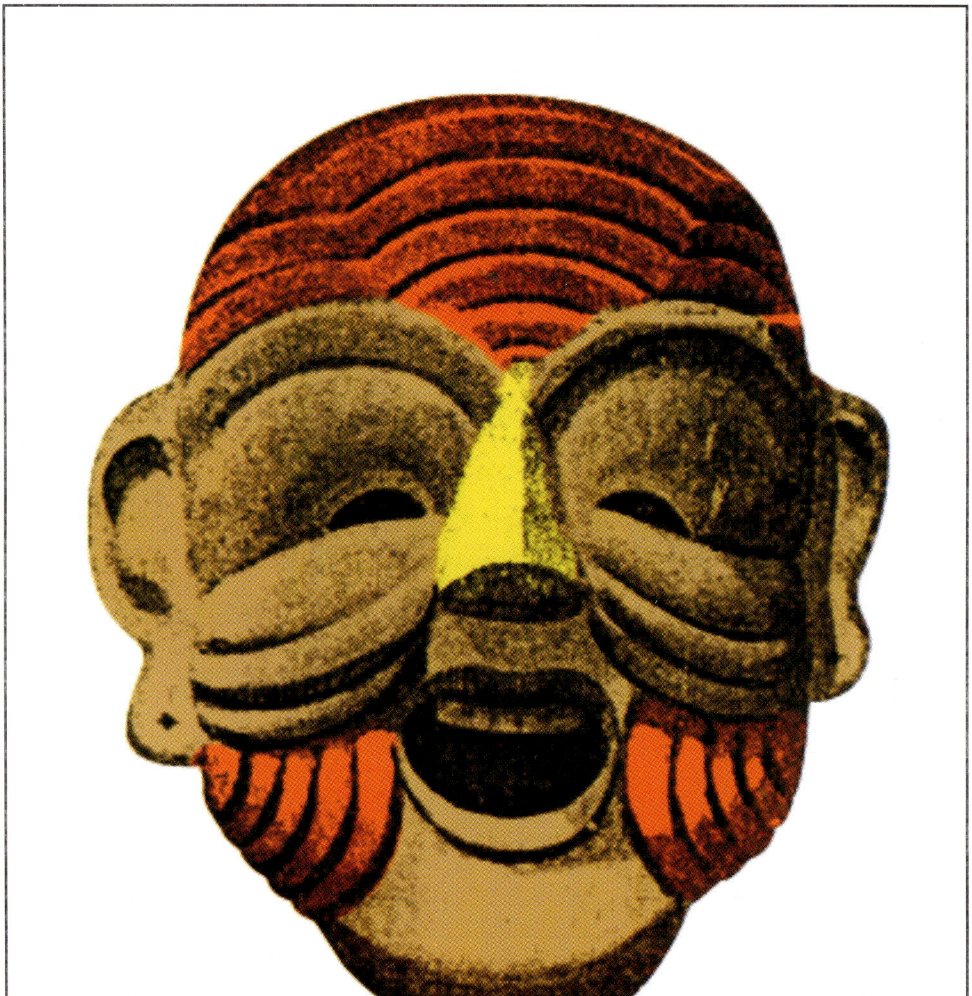

Fig. 47. A Sherthukpen mask.

Fig. 48. Sherthukpen children are timid, shy, cheerful, polite and well behaved.

Fig. 49. Sherthukpens respect the need for space and independence.

Fig. 50. People try to resolve conflicts in a peaceful manner.

Fig. 51. Laam Dema, originally from Rupa, runs her own beauty parlour at Bomdila.

Fig. 52. The young and trendy in Rupa.

Fig. 53. The young women of Rupa.

Let us examine the case of the village Gorwa. The village is mainly populated by Chao families and has only two Thong families. The heads of the two Thong families are both *Gaonburahs*, and the most influential people of the village. They also have the most comfortable homes in the entire village and the only house that has been sanctioned a corrugated sheet in the community is the home of the *Gaonburah*. A gathering of Chao youths said that they do not get any benefits from the administration.

> Benefits are given to those who have good ties with the Rupa Panchayat. We are not educated and cannot even put up our cases in front of the Panchayat. They are big people. If we say something they find offensive, they could punish us with a fine.

This perhaps demonstrates the maintenance of traditional hierarchy and the divide that still exists between the Thongs and the Chaos.

High illiteracy among the Chaos is partly responsible for their continuing plight. Most Thongs are educated because not only are they richer, but also have easier access to schools as they are mainly concentrated in and around the semi-urban settlements. Conversely, the Chaos are not only underprivileged but also have a major geographical disadvantage as they commonly inhabit villages and remote hamlets in the area. No Chao in the history of Gorwa has studied beyond class eight. The village only has one primary school and if a child wishes to study beyond class five, he/she has to go and live in Rupa. The Chaos in Gorwa clearly cannot afford to send their children to Rupa, as a result of which they remain uneducated. This, in turn, implies that they cannot avail of the benefits granted to tribal peoples by the government. If anything, the advent of the monetary economy has left them even poorer and more backward than they ever were. The Thongs, on the other hand, seem to be reaping the benefits of their tribal status. Most Thong children are educated and many are in government service. It could be said that while the rule of the Indian Union has somewhat weakened the dominion of the Thongs over the Chaos, the gap between the rich and poor seems to have grown. And, even today, the Thongs continue to dominate the Chaos, using the power yielded by the state to reinforce the age-old hierarchical order.

It could be of interest to mention here that unlike many of the tribes in Arunachal Pradesh, the Sherthukpen society has no tradition of slavery and the Thongs are not known to have owned slaves like the Adis, Akas, Apa Tanis, Daflas, Gallongs, Mishims or the notorious Singphos and Khamptis. Slavery as an institution, partly a legacy of the political regime of the Ahoms who ruled Assam for about 500 years, and to an extent the British, was practised by the tribes since olden times. However, it was never known to be universal. The Monpas, Sherthukpens and the Noctes do not have any recorded history of slavery. The Ahoms had laid down a system by which a number of families were assigned to predatory tribes who otherwise captured poor Assamese peasants at will, carried them back to their villages and reduced them to slaves. However, slavery among the Arunachali tribes is described as a relatively humane institution by scholars, under which a slave is merely seen as a servant for life.

The institution of slavery was largely seen as a domestic one and a slave was identified with the clan of the master. To site an observation of Dunbar on slavery in the region in 1915,

> From their appearance, it is impossible to distinguish a slave from a free man. The position of a slave who is born of slave parents is more that of a domestic servant, and if a good worker, he will probably be owned by the same master all his life. Slaves live in their owners' houses and are to a certain extent as one of the family.[7]

H.M. Growe, who was the first European to visit the Apa Tani valley in 1889 writes, "Slavery exists in a very mitigated form; slaves are simply servants fed and clothed by their masters and sharing the vicissitudes of their master's fortunes."[8] Consequently, it may be said that the master-slave dynamics among the tribes of Arunachal Pradesh were relatively humane and perhaps not dramatically different from the Thong-Chao relations among the Sherthukpens. As discussed earlier, a number of Chao families were attached to a Thong household for which the Chaos performed compulsory duties and labour.

This may lead us to believe that unlike many tribes of Arunachal Pradesh, the Sherthukpens did not adopt slavery because there already existed a master-servant institution within its social order, and therefore did not lead them to adopt the prevalent trends of other tribes in the region. Perhaps another reason for the Monpas and Sherthukpens to not practise slavery could be their religion—Tibetan Buddhism or Lamaism. However, it is unlikely that their religious ethos could have kept the Sherthukpens away from the institution of slavery because slavery is believed to have existed among the people of Arunachal Pradesh since very early times, while as discussed earlier,[9] Lamaism became widespread among the Sherthukpens only in the past few decades. Therefore, Lamaism could not have influenced the Sherthukpens to either adopt or shun slavery.

The Indian Administration has taken effective measures to abolish slavery in the region and it may be said that today, the institution no longer survives in Arunachal Pradesh, although exceptions to this rule may exist in extremely remote areas. However, as seen in the case of the Sherthukpens, the traditional hierarchy perseveres in a different form, to this day.

MARRIAGE

Several systems of marriage prevail among the people of Arunachal Pradesh. They enter marriage by negotiation or arrangement, service, exchange, capture, purchase and elopement, among other traditions. The Sherthukpens customarily follow the system of marriage by capture; however, today they also practise marriage by negotiation and some cases of marriage by elopement have been known to occur as well. According to *dzizi* Tshering Norbu Dingla, the traditional Sherthukpen marriage was conducted by a *dzizi*. However, today, with the sway of Lamaism, it is the Lama who is the officiating priest in most Sherthukpen marriage alliances.

Class endogamy and clan exogamy are followed. The Thongs do not approve of marriage alliances with the Chaos. The levirate (the practice of marrying the widow of one's childless brother to maintain his line) and sororate (custom of marriage of a man to his wife's sister, usually after the wife has died or proved sterile) are also practised. Parallel and cross-cousin marriages are permitted. However, a boy is not allowed to wed his father's brother's daughter. Monogamy is the general rule. Polyandry or polygamy is not socially acceptable in the Sherthukpen tradition, though rare exceptions exist. Spouses do not have to belong to different settlements and alliances from within the same village are known to occur as well. Widow marriage is permissible but child marriage is disapproved.

Marriage is the most important social occasion in a Sherthukpen family. Marriage ceremonies are important social events which are attended by relatives and friends coming from near and far. This not only helps to widen the social network of the Sherthukpen society but also keeps it well integrated.

A loose form of the *blang* or dormitory system, prevalent in the state and in many tribal belts across the country, still exists in some parts of the Sherthukpen region today. Sharma writes,

> One particular feature of the Sherthukpen life is that young boys and girls do not normally sleep in their own house at night. On attaining puberty, they start sleeping separately with their friends in batches, and thus get opportunities for making love and choosing mates.[10]

The Census of India report notes that, in Rupa,

> There are no separate dormitory buildings. Generally an abandoned house or residential house with surplus accommodation serves as a dormitory... a boy or a girl can join one of the blangs on free-choice; but once one joins a blang one is expected to continue in that till marriage.[11]

From my observation, the dormitory system of the Sherthukpens has become less prominent over the years. Going by the above references, these changes must have eroded the age-old dormitory system of the Sherthukpens in the past few decades rather dramatically, perhaps owing to a decrease in inter-tribal hostility. Das notes,

> A kind of dormitory system for the youth existed among some tribes apparently in response to war needs in the then state of internecine tribal warfare. This dormitory system was also the tribal way of socialisation of the young members. In some cases,

> this institution was found to be on the verge of extinction as it was losing much of its significance with the gradual fading away of inter-tribal hostility during the last century. At peace time, dormitory manpower was treated as part of common village labour which could be deployed for execution of works of common interest.[12]

The extinction of the dormitory system certainly seems most prominent in Rupa where the old dormitory system seems to have perished considerably. However, even in Shergaon, the dormitory system prevails to some extent and it does so to a larger extent in the rural fringes. In Shergaon, the dormitory system is revived every year for a period of 15 days at the event of Chhokar puja. There are three separate mixed (male and female) dormitories for different clans, namely Champo *blang*, Ajilampu *blang* and Thuksima *blang*. The young people congregate in their respective dormitories, drink the local beer, sing, dance and socialise. It is also commonly believed that sexual practices in the dormitories have been somewhat limited in the recent years.

A curious observation with special reference to Rupa, however, is that even today there seems to be a tendency for girls of the same age group to sleep in a group in one of their homes. Also, spending nights at a friend's house is extremely common. This is also observed in the case of boys who move around in groups at night and may visit some of the girls. The young people usually sit around a crackling fire, sipping *phak* or the local beer singing and chating. This friendly and genial interaction, no doubt, helps to initiate some marriage alliances.

Marriage by elopement usually takes place when a couple faces opposition from the parents. This situation may commonly occur in cases of interclass marriages. When a Thong boy elopes with a Chao girl, the boy's parents have to pay a small fine to the girl's father and clan members. The fine is called *sit-zyon*. The boy's parents may then visit the girl's home to formalise the tie and this may be followed by a feast. However, when a Thong girl elopes with a Chao boy, the matter is taken to the village council and a heavy fine is imposed on the father of the boy. The couple is allowed to live as man and wife only after the fine has been paid although no formal ceremonies take place in such a marriage.

At times, if a girl is impregnated, she may be taken to her lover's house by her family and the two are granted social sanction to live as a couple. However, today, legality of marriage is recognised only when it is conducted with certain ceremonies.[13] Interestingly, couples among the tribes in Arunachal Pradesh are occasionally known to wed without any elaborate ceremonial procedure, and this system has stood the test of time and prevailed from the early times.

Dzizi Tanla Thungon of Shergaon, who has also been a *Gaonburah* for the past 25 years and is now 74 years old, said that the fine was paid to the village council in kind when money was not common. An iron stove, or brass and bronze utensils were commonly demanded as fine. The *dzizi* said that when he was young he too had captured a girl who he left after she had a child from him. Tanla Thungon said that they did not have any mutual understanding and she was also much older than him. For his misdemeanour, the *Panchayat* asked him to pay a fine in the form of a horse or its equivalent in gold or silver. Tanla Thungon managed to convince the jury to allow him to separate from his wife and consented to pay the fine imposed on him. His wife too compromised with the situation and the jury allowed them to separate. This event took place about 42 years ago and the issue was eventually settled with a fine of a half acre farmland, a *dao* and a sum of Rs. 26, which was paid by the *dzizi*. The child was also kept by Tanla Thungon.

In the context of marriage to a foreigner, the social approval depends upon the place from where the foreigner originates. Marriage with Nepalese, Bhutanese and Tibetans is frowned upon perhaps because the Nepalese population in the state mainly comprises migrant labourers; the Bhutanese have traditionally been migrants in the area who were granted refuge and thus the Sherthukpens view them as socially subordinate. The Tibetans in the area are mainly refugees and thus landless people. Much like other people who largely live off the land, the Sherthukpens are deeply attached to their land and consider marriage in a landless family as an unworthy proposition. This is so regardless of the fact that the Tibetans are otherwise considered as a culturally refined race. Curiously, I was told that per chance if a Sherthukpen were to marry, say, a European or American, the same superciliousness would not be imposed. Owing to the social affinity shared between the Sherthukpens and Monpas, the Monpas face the least opposition in a marriage alliance with a Sherthukpen. However, broadly, it may be said that Sherthukpens discourage marriage alliances with non-Sherthukpens.

Arranged Marriage or Marriage by Negotiation

If a man wants to enter into a marriage alliance with a particular girl, he first expresses his wish to his parents. If the parents of the boy approve of the girl, they approach the girl's family with a quantity of *phak* or the local beer. If both the parties agree with the alliance, a Lama is consulted and a date chosen for the wedding. According to Dorje Dema Thungchi, of Rupa, a woman is neither informed nor consulted in the matter. However, if she somehow finds out about the matter and is displeased with the match, she may complain to her family members, who in turn try to convince her otherwise. Her caste elders also try to persuade the girl to accept the match. Normally, the girl has to agree to the marriage as her parents have given their word to the boy's parents and going back on it in such matters is considered a matter of shame.

At the time and date prescribed by the Lama, the friends of the boy abduct the girl in question, and carry her away to the boy's house where she is made to stay for a period of three days. It is said that if the girl so desires, she may reject the boy and come back to her parents' home after the period of three days or escape. However, this happens only rarely as, according to some Sherthukpen girls, the society disapproves of any girl who rejects a man after being captured. They were also critical about the system and said that they did not like the tradition of being physically abducted without their will. Interestingly, till some decades ago, the Sherthukpen women wore their hair over their entire face so as not to fall easy prey to capture.

When the news of the girl's capture reaches the parents of the boy, they immediately start preparing for the arrival of the girl. A formal gateway of cane known as *tashi young*[14] is installed at the entrance of the house to welcome the abducted girl. When the news of the capture reaches the family and friends of the girl, and indeed, the news travels like wildfire, the friends of the captured girl are sent with food to the house of the boy by the girl's caste members.[15] The captured girl does not eat a morsel of food from the boy's house and it is said that if she does so, it implies that she has accepted the groom. However, as a tradition even in an arranged marriage where both the groom and bride approve of the match, the girl only eats the food brought to her by her friends. This could be symbolic of the girl's pride and that of her family and clan members.

After two days of the capture, a third caste party representing the boy's side goes to the girl's house and informs her friends and family members about her well-being. This is mainly a gesture to apologise for any discomfort or injury the girl might have received during her abduction.

The Lama is consulted and an auspicious date chosen for the wedding ceremony. A *khiapa*[16] or go-between is selected with great care by the boy's parents. On the day of the wedding, the parents of the groom go to the bride's home in a procession[17] led by the *khiapa* with friends and family of all age groups, carrying with them a yak and a sheep,[18] clothes for the bride's mother and some bronze and brass utensils.[19] The cavalcade led by the *khiapa* is formally received by the father of the bride and presented with the bride price. The yak and sheep are anointed and offered *khatas*.[20]

The procession is welcomed with the exchange of *khatas* and invited in the house and seated in rows, with the groom's side facing the bride's side. The girls from the bride's side get busy serving people with food and drinks. In one of the weddings I attended, the important men from the groom's side were seated in a row on a raised platform. Most men wore Western clothes while almost all the women wore the traditional Sherthukpen dress. A large number of men, and some women, also preferred whiskey to the local beer.

Meanwhile, the bride gets dressed at a clan member's house, and is later brought to her house by her friends. Everyone gathers around in the room and the *dochdo*, or orator, rises and outlines the universality of marriage, saying that girls have to ultimately marry and go and live in the husband's house. The father then tells his daughter that he has made a bargain in which he has lost his daughter, and blesses her. She then seeks blessings from the rest of her family who give her gifts of clothes and bronze and copper utensils. Her mother prays to god to bless her daughter with nine sons and nine daughters. She then turns to her clan members for blessings, who in turn furnish her with gifts of bronze and brass dishes, clothes, traditional Sherthukpen bags, etc. Much like in Hindu marriages, the bride usually remains tearful throughout this session.

The traditional gift of bronze and brass utensils given to the bride by her village and clan members are today being replaced by other household items especially in the semi-urban settlements. This shows a change in the consumption pattern of the Sherthukpens. Also, according to the traditional system, the brother would gift his sister with a horse on her wedding. The horse was the most important animal for the Sherthukpens. In the absence of roads, the horse was the chief means of getting from one place to another and also helped to carry loads to distant places. Today, with the establishment of roads and better communication facilities, the horse has lost its value for the people, and the custom of gifting a horse has been discontinued.

All the gift items are handed over to the *khiapa* who later gives them over to the groom's father after taking a careful account of all the items. The marriage party then leaves with the bride and a few of her close friends, known as *akhyam-rokma*, to the groom's house. The bride is welcomed in her new home by the female members of the clan and village of the groom. The groom's family invites all villagers and clan members for a feast and an atmosphere of merriment prevails. In the wedding I attended in Rupa and Shergaon, the bride was made to sit in a separate room with her friends and other young people. In both cases, flanked by her close friends, the bride usually remains quiet and shy while the other young people in the room indulge in much jest and feasting. The groom has little role in a Sherthukpen marriage and is most conspicuous by his constant absence not only from the bride's home but his parents' house as well.

The *khiapa* hands over the gifts from the bride's side to the groom's family and all the gift items are carefully listed down. The *khiapa* also gives an account of the jewellery either worn by the bride or brought with her as presents. An account of the gifts is maintained by the Sherthukpens because according to their tradition, the ornaments are the property of the parents of the bride and have to be returned to the bride's family by her son after her death. The Census of Indian report notes that,

> according to one informant if the groom during his lifetime kills seven wild boars and presents the heads of the same to the family of his father-in-law, his son or heir is exempted from returning the ornaments of bride in recognition of his bravery, which is a matter of pride for the family of his father-in-law.[21]

The gifts also have to be returned to the bride's family in case of divorce and the details of the gifts have to be produced before the village council.

A Lama is called in to perform the ceremonial rites of marriage. These are brief in nature and highlight the marginal role of religion in a Sherthukpen marriage. As the evening draws near, the atmosphere in the house turns even more festive and the young people sing and dance throughout the night. As mentioned earlier, in the olden times, a Sherthukpen marriage was conducted by a *dzizi*. Today, however, his role is largely replaced by the Lama in the semi-urban settlements. However, in both cases, they only have minor roles to play in marriage. But, in spite of the adoption of Lamaist influences, certain Lo symbols and beliefs have been retained in the modern system of marriage among the Sherthukpens. By way of an example, in the Sherthukpen weddings I attended, large brass vessels full of water floating with *nampling*[22] and rose petals were kept in one corner of the veranda. The *nampling* is considered auspicious in the Lo tradition and is an essential accoutrement in Lo rituals. These petals are similarly placed in a container of water for Lo rituals. Many Sherthukpen gardens also sport strings of *nampling* petals wound around erected pine tree branches that are believed to keep away harmful spirits and engender well-being.

Dzizi Tshering Norbu Dingla of Rupa outlined the role of the *dzizi* in a Sherthukpen wedding. The *dzizi* was first summoned to perform a ceremony before the boy's friends set out to capture the girl. Norbu Dingla said that once the *pooja* or prayer ceremony was successfully performed, it was impossible for the girl to escape. This ceremony, however, was not performed in case of an arranged alliance as it took place in the house of the groom after the bride came in. Small strips of cloth known as *sobong* were placed around the shoulders of the bride and groom. They were then made to sit side by side and the *dzizi* then performed a ceremony. A cane structure a few feet high called *genam* was prepared and covered with a red cloth. The bed of the *genam* was covered with a layer of grain. On this were placed three bowls of silver or wood of different sizes one above the other. The largest bowl at the bottom contained corn, the second was filled with wheat and the bowl at the top was poured with mustard oil. The tradition of building a *genam* during a marriage is still prevalent among the Sherthukpens. One out of the two marriages I attended, at Shergaon, had a beautifully made *genam* in the room where the bride sat with other young people. However, it is difficult to confirm whether the *genam* is indigenous to the Lo or another adoption from Lamaism.

It is interesting to observe that the traditional form of marriage of the Sherthukpens, marriage by capture, has been retained in the more elaborate modern arranged marriage system. However, even today arranged marriages are more prominent only in the semi-urban pockets while the norm in the rural, remote villages is marriage by capture. In the village Gorwa, almost all the marriages take place by capture. No Lamas are called on these occasions and the people seem just as pleased, if not more, with the services of the local *dzizi*. More than any ceremonial proceedings, a marriage is chiefly marked by large-scale feasting and merrymaking not only in the rural pockets, but in the urban settlements as well.

FAMILY

The predominant family type among the Sherthukpens is the nuclear family, followed by the joint family. However, joint families are more an exception than a rule, as recorded by the Census of India report, "Out of 74 households studied, only three are joint families."[23] According to Sherthukpen tradition, a married son makes his own separate residence. The family house may be inherited by the youngest son as the elder sons marry and move to their own homes, in time. However, according to Sharma, who conducted his research in the '60s before the Census of India report, "Joint families are common, though the tendency for such families to break up into separate units has already manifested itself."[24] Curiously, however, Sharma does not, at any time, certify that joint families were a traditional feature in the Sherthukpen social order which was being replaced by the nuclear family system. Perhaps such an assumption comes from the practices of the Indian mainstream rather than the Sherthukpen social order itself. From all the available social patterns, accounts and sources, the nuclear family appears to be the original prominent family-type among the Sherthukpens; however, this cannot be verified owing to the lack of reference material on the Sherthukpens.

The nuclear family is the smallest and most important unit of the Sherthukpen social organisation. It is the economic as well as the participatory unit in all social, religious and public undertakings. Some families may consist of three generations—old parents, the son, his wife and children. At times, a married brother may also live with his unmarried siblings and parents. The Sherthukpens live in a patriarchal society with the head of the family being the father (or the eldest male representative). The father is commonly succeeded by his eldest son as the official and representative head. The role of the head of the family is gradually transferred to the eldest son from the father. Even though the women among the Sherthukpen community may not possess rights of inheritance,[25] they are considered important members of the family unit and the older women in the family play a prominent role in all significant decision making processes of a family. However, it is the father's will that overrides all the important decisions in a Sherthukpen family unit. The father is also the chief provider in a family and it is on him that all responsibilities of his family members lie. He also has to plan and provide for the marriage of each of his children. However, if some siblings have not been settled in the father's lifetime, the responsibility is carried over to the eldest son who inherits the largest share of the father's property and is, thus, in a position to accomplish the duties of his parents. It is also the eldest son who has to perform and bear the expenses of the death rites of the father. However, if, for some reason, the youngest son or another son has been left with the bulk of the inheritance, some of the above-mentioned duties would naturally fall on him. After marriage, sons traditionally remain in the village of the father with their families, but tend to increasingly achieve greater social and economic independence, thereby creating their own niche. Yet, the sons do not achieve absolute independence from their families at least until the father is alive.

Most households are farming units and subsistence from agriculture provides the Sherthukpens with their chief means of livelihood. Whatever labour is available in the family is optimised to cater to the agricultural needs of the family. By studying the social organisation of the Sherthukpens, it can be said that the people endeavour to maximise fulfilment of their labour needs through their social pattern—by birth, marriage, adoption and incorporation. The pattern of levirate, sororate and cross-cousin marriages shows that there is a tendency to retain whatever labour is available within a family. This is rather curious as the need for labour among the Thongs must have been compensated by the readily available free labour of Chaos who traditionally worked for the Thongs. However, these dynamics have somewhat altered today, by the abolishing of the old order and the ready availability of Nepali labourers and servants from the Assamese tribes in the semi-urban settlements of the Sherthukpen belt.

Adoption is allowed in the Sherthukpen social order. The adopted son becomes the son of the foster-father for all practical purposes and is allowed to inherit his property, though not the assets, of his natural father.

Children start participating in minor labour activities at an early age. All these measures serve to maintain the family unit of the Sherthukpens as a viable and independent element of the larger social group, supplementing its labour force by external induction if the need arises.

Division of Labour

The distribution of authority and labour in a Sherthukpen household exists but is highly flexible. There are very few tasks that are either exclusively male or female. As a result, women tend to be more productive and hardworking than their male counterparts. However, it may be said that though flexible, the division of labour among the Sherthukpens is primarily divided on the lines of sex and age.

The domestic work in a Sherthukpen household—drawing water, cooking, cleaning, washing, taking care of the young, animal care, brewing of alcoholic drinks, etc.—is mainly accomplished by women. Agricultural work is fairly mixed though ploughing is essentially a male occupation, as is the felling of trees. Damming and diversion of rivers for irrigation and fishing, hunting and honey collection too are exclusively male occupations. Weaving, spinning and knitting are mainly done by women. Children too start participating in minor labour activities from an early age and take part in collective activities with the other household members.

Inheritance

There is no legal will in the traditional Sherthukpen society. In the old order, the verbal declaration or arrangements made by an individual before his death about his property and debts was regarded as the final word in matters of inheritance. The property of the father is not divided equally among the sons. According to Sharma, the largest portion of the father's property is given to the eldest son while the remaining is divided among the other brothers. Daughters do not traditionally inherit land or immovable property from the father.

If a man passes away without leaving behind any male heir, his property is granted to the nearest male relative. The immovable assets of the father cannot be passed on to the daughter because this overrules clan endogamy and allows the property to move out of the clan. For this reason, it is rare to see any Sherthukpen family without a son, the birth of whom is highly esteemed in each home. A father with no male heir may leave his property to a younger brother or nephew or take a resident son-in-law, who can thus inherit his property. But this is not favoured, owing again to the above-stated rationale. Adopting a child is a more favourable option.

NOTES AND REFERENCES

1. The Yanlaks are also called Yanlos.
2. According to some people, the Yanlaks came to the Sherthukpen territory about nine generations ago.
3. According to the Census of India report, there are only four original clans and not five as has been mentioned by some scholars. The report does not consider Sinchaji to be one of the original clans. The Sherthukpens have conflicting opinions on the subject.
4. *The Sherdukpens* by R.R.P. Sharma (1961), p. 50.
5. *Socio-Economic Survey of Rupa* by Census of India (1971), p. 16.
6. For details, see Religion.
7. *The Abors and Gallongs* by G.D.S. Dunbar (1915), p. 60.
8. *Mr. Crowe's Account of a Journey to Apa Tani Country* by A.M. Crowe, Foreword, p. 1.
9. For details, see Religion.
10. *The Sherdukpens* by R.R.P. Sharma (1961), pp. 55-56.
11. *Socio-Economic Survey of Rupa* by Census of India (1971), p. 50.
12. *Tribes of Arunachal Pradesh in Transition* by Gurudas Das (1995), p. 25.
13. *Socio-Economic Survey of Rupa* by Census of India (1971), p. 51.
14. The cane gateway or *tashi young* is perhaps a Lamaist adoption. Monasteries and other places of religious importance often support such a gateway. These structures can also be spotted at the entrance of towns and villages in Arunachal Pradesh as well as other parts of the north-east. However, the gateways are a common feature in Nagaland, which today is mainly Christian.
15. The friends of the bride may belong to any caste.
16. The *khiapa* is usually an elderly man well versed with all the intricacies of marriage customs and rites, and known for his fine speech and mannerism. He is the chief arbiter in a Sherthukpen

wedding. His role is comparable to that of the *bek-bo* or go-between of the Lepchas of Sikkim.

17. The marriage procession consists of the immediate family of the groom, his uncle, other clan members as well as the Chaos attached to the groom's clan. Traditionally, the Chaos carried with them large quantities of local beer or *phak*. The *phak* would be consumed in great quantities by the people, especially in cases when the journey from the groom's to the bride's house was a long one. The bride price or the yak and sheep is also carried along with the procession.
18. According to the Sherthukpen tradition, the gift of a yak and sheep is the fixed bride price which is given to all the clan members of the bride. A yak and a sheep are traditionally the bride price for the wealthy Sherthukpens; the less privileged people, however, gift the girl's clan with a sheep. The yak and sheep are traditionally said to be bartered for the girl and thus the bride does not partake of the meat from the animals paid as bride price.
19. Bronze and brass utensils are traditionally given as gifts in Sherthukpen marriages. These dishes were earlier purchased from the foothill *haat* bazaars of Assam. The Sherthukpens have trade and barter relations with the Kachari Bodo tribes of the foothills since ancient times. Bronze and brass utensils of different sizes are commonly found in almost every Sherthukpen home.
20. A *khata* is a scarf which is commonly used by the Sherthukpens and is symbolic of honouring someone. They use the *khata* much like the neighbouring Monpas or the Lepchas and Bhutias of Sikkim and is perhaps a Tibetan Lamaist influence.
21. *Socio-Economic Survey of Rupa* by Census of India (1971), p. 58.
22. The *nampling* is perhaps the white poppy or is a flower closely resembling the poppy. My fieldwork took place in the winter so I was unable to see any *nampling* plants. However, poppy was widespread in the region and was of great value to the people of Arunachal Pradesh. A large number of Arunachali tribes were known to be addicted to opium. The connection between intoxicants and religious practices is an ancient global phenomenon and is especially prevalent among tribal faiths and practices across the world.
23. *Socio-Economic Survey of Rupa* by Census of India (1971), p. 138.
24. *The Sherdukpens* by R.R.P. Sharma (1961), p. 52.
25. There have been rare instances of daughters inheriting land and property from the father but these are based on individual discretion and are more an exception than a rule among the Sherthukpens.

3

Socio-Political System

SOCIO-POLITICS

> It is axiomatic that whenever the Central Government is strong and effective, the people tend to lose their self reliance and lean heavily on the Government. In India's recent history, which is crowded with centuries of alien rule exercised from the Centre, there has been gradual decay of the age-old village authority which in ancient times used to manage the affairs at the village and community levels. Happily in the North East Frontier Agency, the inherent urge of its people to take stock of their problems and deal with them has remained in tact. The daily humdrum of life in NEFA is by and large, managed by its own people who over the past centuries have come to evolve their own codes and customary laws to adjust over disputes and the sharing of Nature's resources available to them.[1]
>
> *P.N. Luthra, Adviser to the Governor of Assam, Shillong, 1965.*

Verrier Elwin was the chairman of a committee appointed by the Ministry of Home Affairs to evaluate the working of what in 1959 were known as Special Multipurpose Tribal Blocks. Based on the countrywide research conducted for the purpose and his exhaustive work in Arunachal Pradesh, he outlines certain common features of the tribal councils in Arunachal Pradesh in one of his books.

It is perhaps of some merit to examine the common features of village councils in Arunachal Pradesh before discussing in detail the Sherthukpen Council. Elwin notes,

> They (tribal councils) all derive their authority from ancient times and the fact that they are the expression of the will and power of the whole people. They are supported not only by social, but also by supernatural, sanctions... All the councils are informal in character and except for the Monpa councils and the Adi bangos, which seem to be more highly organised, the conception of regular membership, committees, secretaries and so on has not come in. The people composing the councils are the accepted leaders of a village and always include the local priest, whose services are often required, and, of course, the officially appointed headmen who are issued with red coats... Decisions are not taken by a formal vote but discussion continues until general unanimity is achieved.
>
> The functions of the village council are threefold—judicial, administrative and developmental. On the judicial side the councils settle the disputes within the village boundaries and considerable powers have been given to them under the Assam Frontier (Administration of Justice) Regulation of 1945. Even serious crimes against tribal society (but not against Government) have been and are being settled, generally to the satisfaction of all concerned, by these councils. Probably, to the tribal mind, this is the most important of the council's functions.
>
> On the administrative side, the councils deal with the maintenance of paths and bridges; they see to the water-supply and sanitation of a village; they fix the dates of communal hunting and fishing and decide when the main agricultural operations should take place and when festivals should be held. Some of them make it their business to care for the poor and the disabled. There is no rule about this, and much depends upon the nature of the leading men of any particular council. Similarly, with regard to development, this depends largely on the extent to which the local officials have worked through the local councils... generally, when the council as such is approached by an official, the response is enthusiastic.
>
> The 1945 Regulation has already limited the type of 'punishment' that can be inflicted, and in fact the heavy punishments of former days have already almost entirely disappeared. Girls may still have their hair cut for immorality,

but they are no longer stripped naked and beaten. Offenders are no longer buried alive, rolled over cliffs, or pushed into rivers to drown; already, of their own accord, the people have adopted the system of compensation, which in practice is adjusted to the wealth and position of the accused.

The policy of the NEFA Administration is to accept this situation and to strengthen the councils and work through them. Great care, however, has hitherto been taken not to over-administer the councils and make them conform to our idea...[2]

In the pre-independence times, however, Elwin notes,

The policy of Government in the pre-independence period was to attempt no more than a skeleton administration in the foothills; to send out punitive expeditions in reaction to the more serious raids; to impose blockades and establish fortified posts at strategic points; and in certain cases to pay what is called posa to the Chiefs on condition that they kept their people under control.[3]

The Sherthukpen society was traditionally governed by a central administrative council based in their mother village of Rupa, which has, since long, been the nucleus of the Sherthukpen society. The Sherthukpens are a small tribe of about 5,000 people. Being small in number, it is possible to mobilise the people under the local centralised governance from Rupa which controls the social, political and administrative life of the people. Shergaon has had its own village council although it is not as formal or organised as that of Rupa. Originally, however, Shergaon is believed to have been affiliated to the council at Rupa but with time the people of Shergaon started to solve their administrative problems internally and stopped coming to Rupa.

Today, most sizable villages have their own village councils called *jung* headed by the popularly elected headman or *Gaonburah*. The *Gaonburah* system prevailed in the area when Arunachal Pradesh or NEFA, as it was earlier known, as well as other north-eastern states were a part of the territory of Assam. The *Gaonburahs* were chosen with the council of the British authorities when they took over from the Ahom kings in the early 19th century.[4] The village council of the

Sherthukpens handles the internal administration of a village and most petty disputes are resolved by the council. Nawan Norbu Khrimie, who has been a *Gaonburah* in Rupa for the past two years, informed me that *Gaonburah* is an Assamese word coined by the British. The Sherthukpens earlier addressed the *Gaonburah* as *Theekakhaw,* which in Sherthukpen means 'the head of the village'.

There were no *Gaonburahs* in the villages or *pams* (hamlets) during the British rule. The *busties* were administered from Rupa. Grievances were heard in the *gompa* and all disputes were settled from here. According to the *Gaonburah* at Rupa, the British and the *Goanburahs* would choose Jungme Akhaw (Active Members, or literally, Meeting Elders) who assisted the *Gaonburahs* in the village operations. In time, *Gaonburahs* were not just limited to Rupa but also began to be chosen to represent smaller villages and *pams* in the area. The first *Gaonburah* from Jigaon was chosen about 30 years ago. At Thungri, the first *Gaonburah* was selected about 15 years ago and in the villages and *pams* of Gorbow, Chillipam, Lingbaktang, Dikshi, Mimbachhur and Mukhuthing, the first *Gaonburahs* were picked out only about six years ago. However, the first *Gaonburah* chosen outside of Rupa was at Shergaon. This must have taken place many years ago as no one could furnish the details of the period of the selection of the first *Gaonburah* at Shergaon.[5]

Other office-bearers are the *Jungme* or ordinary members and *Kachung* or watch-keepers, who are all selected on an honorary basis. The *Kachung* performs the duty of a guard and is also referred to as *Chowkidar*. Their duty is to patrol the village at night, convey (shout out) any orders from the administration or village council and assist the *Gaonburahs* and other members in their endeavours. But the weight of authority lies with the *Gaonburahs* whose decision is taken as paramount. The office of the *Gaonburah* is not hereditary; however, there is a common tendency to elect new *Gaonburahs* from the families of the old *Gaonburahs*. Therefore, the sons or brothers of the *Gaonburah* stand a good chance to be future *Gaonburahs*. Netan Dorje Thongon, aged 34, is the young *Gaonburah* of Doimara. He was nominated to the post in 2003 and has succeeded his father who was the *Gaonburah* of Doimara since 1982. I did not come across any *Gaonburah* in the entire Sherthukpen belt who was from the Chao community and could not find any reference to one in the past who belonged to the less privileged clan. People were of the opinion that *Gaonburahs* came only from the Thong clans. The same pattern was observed for the post of *Jungme* and only the post of the *Kachung* has members from the Chao clan. This is true in spite of the fact that in the recent years, there have been a small number of people from the Chao community who are now officers in the Arunachal administration. But the clan rigidity is such that even during festivals like *Khiksaba* all the Chaos are made to sit at a level below the Thongs, irrespective of their economic or educational background. However, apart from the inherent rigidity, such occasions are carried out in a cordial manner and there is no overt exhibition of Thong superiority apart from what has ritually and traditionally existed through the ages.

The *jung* has traditionally played a central role in every sphere of Sherthukpen life, including the social, political, administrative, judicial as well as the economic affairs of the people. Each village council is represented by one (or more) headman or *Gaonburah* who, with the assistance of other office-bearers, runs and controls the village administration according to the indigenous law. Das outlines the functions of the *Gaonburah* in pre-industrial Arunachal Pradesh,

> All land in a village, theoretically, was common village land under the management of the Village Council or the Village Chief. The Gaonburah or the Chief, as the leader of the village, used to decide which plots were to be brought under jhumming, when agricultural operation would be undertaken, when and where would hunting or fishing be done, etc. In the matter of common interest like construction of village road, bridge, houses for common use, etc., the village head used to mobilise the communal labour in this regard. Thus, in the absence of any separate economic institutions, economic activities were also organised by the tribal socio-political organisations.[6]

The names of the chosen *Gaonburahs* have to be cleared by the administration as the *Gaonburahs* are also the representatives of the government at the village level. It is also the duty of the *Gaonburah* to inform the villagers of government orders as and when this may be required. The *Gaonburahs* are each given a red coat by the government, symbolic of their link with the administration. It is common to have more than one *Gaonburah* in a village. However, the *Gaonburahs* are ranked by number—*Gaonburah* 1, *Gaonburah* 2, *Gaonburah* 3. The ultimate authority remains with *Gaonburah* 1. Even so, the tradition of discussion till such time that a consensus has been achieved is still the norm and this approach perhaps helps contain power struggles and one-upmanship.

Haimendorf writes, "Individual tribal groups have made different arrangements for the establishment of a system of social controls which interlock with the existing framework of the government administration."[7] The Sherthukpen system of administration has been evolved to encompass both the traditional village council, i.e. the *Gaonburah* setup as well as the Indian law, order and administration establishments. The role of the Panchayat is limited in the area and the Panchayat comes in primarily in financial matters, mainly for the purpose of developmental and construction works. However, the Panchayat members, some officers from the Rupa administration as well as the *Gaonburahs* and other members together preside over the important meetings held in the Rupa monastery. These are usually held in the *gompa* grounds on sunny days or inside the *gompa* during the harsh winter.

Voting is held but in 2003, all the seats in Rupa were uncontested, although in Shergaon there was reported to be a 'tough fight'. Nevertheless, with the introduction of the Indian electoral system, certain corruptions of the traditional order have been perceived.

The Sherthukpen youth in the area have also mobilised a youth alliance called the Sherthukpen Youth Association under which the Sherthukpen girls and boys, mainly from the educated semi-urban settlements, organise cultural and sports events. These events engender a mutual bond among the Sherthukpen youth and add momentum to the proliferation of indigenous traditions of song and dance. The Sherthukpen

Youth Association was believed to be most active in the 80s when the youth in the organisation released cassettes of Sherthukpen songs and did many other activities to promote Sherthukpen culture. A sizable thrust to the Youth Association comes from the district headquarters of Bomdila. There are no college-level educational institutions in the entire Sherthukpen belt, hence after school many of the Sherthukpens go to Bomdila for further studies where youth activities are mobilised.

Traditionally, although the office of the *Gaonburah* is not hereditary but once elected, the *Gaonburah* would remain in power till he becomes too old to continue with his duties. Sharma writes, "As a rule, once elected, the Gaonburah holds office for life or until he becomes infirm."[8] However, today, the *Gaonburahs* in the Sherthukpen belt, and, perhaps in the entire state, are frequently swapped with a change in the state ministry. Each politician comes with his own entourage of supporters. The Minister of State D.K. Thongdok sees this as a natural evolution of the times. He says,

> the Gaonburah or any other person is directly or indirectly involved in politics today. Earlier, the Gaonburah members were even more actively involved in the politics of Arunachal Pradesh. A Gaonburah in the 70s, Netan Dorjee was the Zila Parishad member in the 70s.

As already discussed, *Gaonburahs* are extremely influential at the village level and thus attract a sizeable political clout. The people of Arunachal Pradesh are well aware of the local politics and gains that accompany such affiliations. Many people are actively involved in politics.

After the Chinese troops invaded Arunachal Pradesh, there was a great spurt of activity by the Indian administration to accelerate the pace of development. Roads were laid down across the territory of Arunachal Pradesh and even the remote and isolated pockets were connected. The ideology of the Indian Administration too witnessed a decisive shift from the Nehru-Elwin Policy[9] of tribal revivalism and protectionism to a policy of integration, immediately after the Sino-Indian border conflict. This radical change in perspective was pursued aggressively after 1972. NEFA was declared a Union Territory of India under the new name of Arunachal Pradesh in 1972. The first election to the Legislative Assembly was held in 1980, which paved the way for party line politics. The imposition of parliamentary democracy upon the indigenous village councils of the tribal areas and the seeping of party politics cutting across the ethnic boundaries disturbed the age-old equations substantially. The interest of the elite of the old order was left unhampered and they were largely accommodated into the new framework to ensure least retaliation or protest while the changes were being implemented. The restructuring carried on till it was significantly consolidated in 1987 and the Union Territory of Arunachal Pradesh was granted statehood. English and Hindi were pursued in schools and added thrust was given towards popularising Hindi and Hindu missions.[10] Das writes,

> Since 1972, this policy of aggressive integration has been implemented at such an extensive scale that the line of demarcation between assimilation and integration gets blurred.[11]

The Minister of State D.K. Thongdok, after coming to power in 1999, claims that he has helped add greater impetus towards the revival of the age-old *Chhatpu Nsey* or the Thukpen Village Council (TVC) at Rupa, held every three years since its revival in 1990. The main function of the *Chhatpu Nsey* is to discuss criminal cases which are debated at length under various sections, and the guilty penalised under the various sections laid down by the council. The procedures of the *Chhatpu Nsey* persist for a period of three days to one week every three years.

The *Chhatpu Nsey* was revived in 1990 and the last (and fifth) *Chhatpu Nsey* was held in 2002. The council is believed to be based on the ancient administrative system of the Sherthukpens, which has now been implemented with changes in tune with the present day. The Thukpen Village Council includes in its folds the administration of Rupa and the surrounding villages of Thungri, Brokpu Blong, Jungpam, Gorbow, Diksi, Mukuthing, Mimbachhur, Jigaon, Musaksing, Lingbaktang and Chillipam. The *Gaonburah*, a Council Secretary, Members and the *Khomi*, or households, form the *Chhatpu Nsey* committee.

Nawan Norbu Khrimie, a *Gaonburah* of Rupa for the past two years,[12] said that the Sherthukpens earlier addressed the *Gaonburah* as *Theekakhaw*, which in Sherthukpen means 'the head of the village'. Norbu Khrimie said that there was no voting involved in the selection of the *Gaonburah*. However, the selection process was based on a unanimous decision taken by the villagers based on the capability of the concerned individual. Khrimie said that it was only the Thongs or the more privileged clan members of Rupa who participated in the selection of the *Gaonburah*. The Chaos were not involved in the procedure. This illustrates that the administrative organisation of the Sherthukpens has not evolved into a more democratic or egalitarian practice. Even today, it is the Thongs or the higher class that make all the important decisions related to Sherthukpens at large, while the underprivileged Chaos continue to remain outside the democratic realms and do not participate substantially either in the democratic institutions or democratic practices prevalent among the Sherthukpen Thongs. However, this certainly does not indicate that nothing has changed. There are marked indications to illustrate that change has indeed swept in.

The indigenous law of the Sherthukpens has worked since ancient times; and according to Sharma,

> The village councils are popular as they provide speedy justice. They also enjoy and often restore goodwill between the opposing parties. Even when the parties cannot be persuaded to come to a compromise, the awards of the village council are in consonance with the traditions and conventions of the people.[13]

However, the indigenous law of the Sherthukpens in the present times leaves some aspects to be desired. On the face of it, the Thongs and Chaos have a fairly cordial relationship but some frustrations with the present order can be perceived and change is being embraced or swallowed, as the case may be, and internalised gradually. During my fieldwork, I spent a substantial amount of time among Sherthukpen women and noticed that it is not uncommon for Thong girls to have friends among the Chao community, However, both are certainly aware of the differences in their clans and due to years of servitude, the Chao girls would, at times, automatically carry the bags of the Thong girls walking with them. This behaviour was also internalised by the Thong girls who would often not be able to decipher that anything was amiss. At times, some Thong girls would object to Chao girls carrying their bags and then they would together laugh off the matter.

Perhaps the most significant shift is observed in the level of awareness of not only the Chaos but the Thongs as well. Both are aware that discrimination with impunity is no longer the law under a democratic rule. There also seems to be a palpable sense of discontentment among the smaller villages and *pams* for the centralised dominion of the Rupa council. In the 5th *Chhatpu Nsey*, the people of Jigaon had appealed for the following:

> **Appeal from Jigaon**[14]
> The public of Jigaon and Musaksing villages requested the TVC to exempt them from the following:
> *Chhokok Tep-khan* during Wang[15] (Lamaist blessing ceremony)
> *Yokmu-kho Sat-khan*[16] (Tax collection by *Gaonburah*)
> Blu-blaat[17] (Community work group)

They[18] also proposed to perform *Chhokor* and *Wang* at Jigaon on their own.

After a prolonged discussion, the Council[19] gave the following decision.

If any village wishes to perform *Chhokor/Wang* in their village, the Council cannot prevent them from doing so. However, the age-old system of contribution to TVC by each household in the form of *Chhokok-khomi tep-khan, Yokmu-kho, Kho-satkhan,* etc. cannot be exempted.

At the most, certain *Blu-blaat* can be exempted to certain villages if at all they are not able to attend the TVC *Blu-blaat* due to their own village *Blu-blaat*.

This illustrates that there is a growing demand by the smaller Sherthukpen settlements for the TVC to decentralise authority and allow individual villages to conduct their own business. When I questioned some members of the TVC, an explanation given was that the people of Jigaon have an 'ego hassle' being affiliated to the TVC as a number of important officials belong to the village of Jigaon like the Chief Engineer, Inspector General of the North-East Zone, etc. A certain tension with the people of Jigaon in connection with other Sherthukpens can be felt. This could be owing to the early history of the people of Jigaon who were migrants from Bhutan and were later assimilated within the Chaos as a distinct community. However, this would also be insufficient explanation because the same discontentment can also be perceived among the people of other villages, who are not as well placed as the people of Jigaon and cannot even put their cases before the TVC for fear of being penalised. A gathering of Chao youth in Gorwa said that they do not get any benefits from the administration.

> Benefits are given to the people who have good ties with the people in the Rupa Panchayat. We are not educated and cannot even put up our cases in front of the Panchayat. They are big people. If we say something they find offensive, they could punish us with a fine.

This clearly demonstrates the maintenance of the traditional hierarchy and the divide that still exists between the Thongs and Chaos. This illustrates a growing resentment among the less privileged to be held answerable before an unsympathetic council riddled with hierarchy and red tape. Another accusation among the poorer sections was that only those people benefit who have good connections with the people in the Rupa Panchayat. Therefore, the people also suspect a certain amount of corruption in the dealings of the TVC and the Panchayat. Under the state-run machinery and in Arunchal Pradesh, the near absence of private investment corruption is gradually being accepted as part and parcel of everyday reality.

This is not to say that people do not see the salient features of their indigenous law. Indeed, it is not uncommon to hear Sherthukpens speaking in glorifying terms about their law. Many are of the opinion that their local law and order policies engender harmony and reinforce the laws laid down by their ancestors. Punishments and fine are often seen as a tool to bolster tradition and morality as well as to discourage straying individuals.

COMMUNITY LIVING

The Sherthukpen society has a fine network of labour groups based on the principle of mutual exchange, and this exchange of assistance is common to the Sherthukpen everyday life. Each family is a part of these mutual help groups. The assistance is well reciprocated and is seen as an investment. It is interesting to note that none of these mutual aid groups are based along clan or kinship lines. Extended families may be extremely important, but in day-to-day matters, it is these mutual aid groups that are relied upon. This also enumerates how obligations to the family, village, public institutions, neighbours, aid-groups and friends act as the paramount force that unites the community and connects the family unit to a larger group or community. The communal work groups of the Sherthukpens are still largely in operation and thus can be documented. However, I could come across no written references to the collaborative work groups of the Sherthukpens.

BLU-BLAAT

Blu-blaat is the most prominent collaborative work group institution of the Sherthukpens. Households of the village or *pam* also contribute to the larger public enterprises of the village as well as to the welfare institutions. This collective group works for community welfare like the upkeep of paths, construction of bridges, *gompa* repairs, construction of schools or community buildings, etc., and is mobilised by the *Gaonburah* or the village council. *Blu-blaat* is organised from the village and a member of each household contributes towards the common cause. Those found missing from *Blu-blaat* without a valid excuse may be fined with a quantity of *phak* for the people who have successfully performed their duties. A person is responsible for extracting fine from those missing during communal labour without a valid reason. In Rupa, I heard the story of one Pema Dorje who was assigned this task in the 70s and was such an expert in extracting the fine that he is remembered in Rupa to this day. I was told that if someone tried to shrug away from paying the fine, Pema, more popularly known as Penzay, would go to the person's house and pick up an expensive article and not return it till such time that the requisite amount of *lopani* was served to all the people who had performed the communal labour.

A poor Sherthukpen may also summon help from this collective labour group by approaching the *Gaonburah* with some *lopani* and divulging his problems to him. If the *Gaonburah* is of the opinion that the individual genuinely needs extra assistance, he may mobilise the work group in aid of the poor individual in his endeavours. The collaborative work group culture cuts through the boundaries of different neighbourhoods and age differences, as a wide range of age groups participate in the common activities. All such errands are voluntary in nature; contributions and chores are compulsory and are given out to families on a rotation basis.

Brampu

This labour group, which engages all the families of the village, is mainly sought for agricultural help or for the construction of houses. Help is summoned by a member of the family that requires extra labour. A member of the family goes to individual families and asks for help in accomplishing the task at hand. However, help is first sought from one's clan members and then from other families in the community or village.

Haaphak tepa

The literal meaning of *haa* is food, *phak* is *lopani* or the local beer and *tepa* is Sherthukpen for help or assistance. *Haaphak Tepa* is mainly organised at the death of an individual. The Lamaist rituals pertaining to death are extremely elaborate and require high expenditure from the family of the dead. After the death of a person a Lama is required to perform elaborate rituals for the first seven days and on the 7th day *chok*[20] or *prasaad* is distributed to the entire community. *Chok* is also distributed on the 14th, the 21st and the 49th day and after a year of the death. On each of these days, a Lama is called in to perform elaborate rituals pertaining to death. At such times, *Haaphak Tepa* assistance is offered by other households to the family of the dead in the form of foodgrains, *phak*, food, vegetables, wood, etc. so as to ease the financial burden on the family of the dead.

Kaching Pa

The Sherthukpen society has an age-old system of internal security. It must be remembered that the tribes in Arunachal Pradesh were often engaged in inter-tribal warfare and internal security was one of the chief concerns of the various tribes that inhabited this rugged mountainous terrain. Although the same security concerns no longer exist in Arunachal Pradesh today, the Sherthukpens, long used to their indigenous system of security, continue to practise it today as well. The *Kaching Pa* are voluntary guards that stay up the entire night and conduct security perambulations in the various settlements of the Sherthukpen belt. The *Kaching Pa* are organised according to different clans. The nine Sherthukpen clans are mobilised clan-wise to provide for the internal security of the Sherthukpens.

Jooyooum Bu

This co-operative work group is another organisation for internal security, which mainly involves the voluntary employment of the young men of the community. *Jooyooum Bu* was similar to *Kaching Pa* but was a more aggressive system of internal security that required the guards to maintain constant vigil and keep a watch from various strategic spots that facilitate easy spotting of troubling elements. This was fundamental to the security of the Sherthukpens during earlier times when they were under the constant onslaught of the warring Akas. The neighbouring Akas, known for their prowess in inter-tribal feuds and warfare, would come in droves and raid entire Sherthukpen villages and *pams* carrying away whatever they could find of any value, including Sherthukpen women. *Jooyooum Bu* is no longer organised today as the threat earlier perceived from the raiding neighbouring tribes does not exist any longer.

Yanpo blu

Apart from the above-mentioned groups, a person's friends also formulate a co-operative system. These friends who may or may not belong to the same village or clan get together and formulate a common fishing party. The friends get together and go fishing for an entire night at planned intervals. The duties are rotated and fish consumed by all present and the leftovers are distributed equally that are taken back to the individual families. Fishing is mainly a male task and as such this group too mainly comprises Sherthukpen men. Mutual friendship is the only basis for this co-operative grouping and in times of hardship, may include the offer of help and material objects and services from friends, apart from a measure of psychological support. This help group is distinct from other co-operative groups as it is less formal and no grave reciprocal obligations are prerequisites of this exchange.

Sapo bla

This system of collaborative labour is similar to the *Yanpo Blu* but instead of fishing, it involves hunting led by members participating in this co-operative group.

CONFLICT RESOLUTION AND DECISION-MAKING

The Sherthukpens have since long been known for their mild and friendly mannerism among the tribes of Arunachal Pradesh. Crime among the Sherthukpens is, and has been, rare; strong disagreements are socially disapproved, violence or aggressive behaviour is discouraged and theft is highly unusual. People seldom lock their homes in the Sherthukpen belt, except in the semi-urban settlements; the architecture of a typical Sherthukpen house does not cater to any foolproof locking system. The slide-lock on the indigenous Sherthukpen main door can easily be opened by anyone from both inside as well as outside the house. Earlier, threat was perceived largely from outside the tribe and not typically from within it. However, if crime did take place, it was strictly dealt with under the sections laid down in the Sherthukpen canon.

If a Sherthukpen makes a complaint to the *Gaonburah* which, according to the *Gaonburah,* deserves to be addressed, he summons the village council to discuss the breach of trust. The two parties are brought in front of the village council and are allowed to explain themselves freely. The case is then discussed at length till such time that a unanimous decision surfaces which, if approved by the *Gaonburah*, largely prevails. The judgement is given by the *Gaonburah* at the end of the discussions. However, if one of the parties is unhappy with the outcome, he may approach the administration for further probing and investigation. Today, most disputes are settled in this manner and the most common form of punishment is a fine imposed on the guilty. Traditionally, however, some disputes were also settled by, what Sharma terms as, "oath or ordeal".[21]

He writes,

> Oath and ordeal, through which the aid of supernatural agencies is invoked, are resorted to when the ordinary methods of ensuring justice fail. The accused may prove his innocence to the council by offering a scarf in the name of the local deity and swearing 'if I am responsible for the crime, blood will come out of my nose within three days. If no blood comes out during the period, the complainant has not only to drop the charge, but also to give compensation to the accused in the shape of cash or kind'.[22]

Haimendorf discerned a grudge among the older people of Arunachal Pradesh[23] (Nishis and Hill Miris) with the administration for softening and banning some of the harsher punishments and the resultant loss in the indigenous morality,

> Some old men deplore the abolishment of certain punishments which used to be inflicted on offenders. Thus Taba Tat, a former government interpreter and incidentally the father-in-law of the present Education Minister, did not hold back with his criticism of the "soft" attitude of the government towards those guilty of adultery and abduction. "Previously", he told me, "a man who had run away with another man's wife would have been caught, and if he was unable to pay compensation, he would have been cut into pieces. Now cases of abduction and elopement have increased because neither men nor wives are any longer afraid. If government wants to reduce the frequency of such occurrences,

> we should be permitted to cut the offenders pieces as it was done in the old days... Though Taba Tat expressed these conservative views, we have seen that in his own family affairs he had acted with remarkable tolerance and liberality.[24]

The Census of India report also discusses execution of justice by the method of 'oath and ordeal' that involves similar superstitions. However, this method of establishing the law is not widespread in the Sherthukpen belt today. As mentioned earlier, today the *Gaonburah* presides over these meetings which are also attended by the Panchayat members as well as representatives from the Rupa administration and other prominent members of the village. In the remote areas, it is the village council and the *Gaonburahs* who administer justice. Here, the method of oath and ordeal is practised at times when the *Gaonburah* and the village council both are of the opinion that the dispute could benefit from supernatural intervention and the local priest or *dzizi* is called in for paranormal intervention. However, being a small tribe, the Sherthukpens are centralised under the Rupa leadership, who discuss matters of importance that take place in the entire Sherthukpen belt apart from those of Shergaon, as it has its own judicial and administrative body. An overall assessment of the law and order situation takes place every three years during the *Chhatpu Nsey*.

NOTES AND REFERENCES

1. *Democracy in NEFA* by Verrier Elwin (1988), Foreword.
2. *Democracy in NEFA* by Verrier Elwin (1988), pp. 18-23.
3. *Myths of NEFA* by Verrier Elwin (1958), Introduction, p. xvi.
4. The Ahoms ruled over Assam till 1826, the date of the British annexation.
5. The number of years may not be exact and are only approximate in nature. They have been taken from various *Gaonburahs* of the Sherthukpen belt.
6. *Tribes of Arunachal Pradesh in Transition* by Gurudas Das (1995), p. 62.
7. *Highlanders of Arunachal Pradesh: Anthropological Research in North-East India* by Christoph von Fürer-Haimendorf (1982), p. 118.
8. *The Sherdukpens* by R.R.P. Sharma (1961), p. 69.

9. The term Nehru-Elwin Policy refers to the rapid expansion of administration under the former revivalist-protectionist approach. The policy endeavoured to achieve changes amidst least intervention in the socio-political autonomy, tribal traditions, arts and a protectionist-welfare approach towards economic development of the tribes of Arunachal Pradesh. The framework of the policy was originally framed by the Bordoloi Committee. The committee formulated the policy for the Partially Excluded Areas under undivided Assam, mainly formulated on the basis of the Report of the North East Frontier (Assam) Tribal and Excluded Areas Sub-Committee headed by G.N. Bordoloi.
10. *Tribes of Arunachal Pradesh in Transition* by Gurudas Das (1995), pp. 75-90.
11. Ibid., p. 92.
12. Rumour has it that *Gaonburah* Nawan Norbu Khrimie acquired the post after the coming to power of the Minister at Rupa.
13. *The Sherdukpens* by R.R.P. Sharma (1961), p. 72.
14. Taken from the printed extracts of The 5th *Chhatpu Nsey*, 2002.
15. Lamaist blessing ceremony.
16. The collection of tax by the *Gaonburahs* and members from various blocks or *chhokoks*.
17. *Blu-blaat* is a community workgroup. For details, see Community Living in this chapter.
18. Here, *They* stands for Jigaon.
19. The Council stands for the Thukpen Village Council or TVC.
20. Chok is a *prasaad* or blessed food that consists of an assortment of vegetables, rice and *phak* or the local beer.
21. *The Sherdukpens* by R.R.P. Sharma (1961), p. 70.
22. Ibid., p. 71.
23. His comments here are mainly in reference to the Nishis and the Hill Miris. However, I am using the above quote to represent a sentiment that is not necessarily limited to the two tribes but is indicative of a more widespread view.
24. *Highlanders of Arunachal Pradesh: Anthropological Research in North-East India* by Christoph von Fürer-Haimendorf (1982), p. 118.

4

Economy

The velocity of change is accelerating. This is not only true for the busy cosmopolitan cities ever swarming with consumers but even more so for people and communities who have been long estranged from the rest of the world owing to the dynamics of geography, politics and culture. The Sherthukpens, much like the neighbouring Monpas, Buguns (Khowas), Hrussos (Akas) and Dhamaais (Mijis), procured the necessities of life like salt, matchsticks, cloth, etc. through trade and barter. For centuries tribal life in the region whirled around slash and burn farming without any significant shift in their internal socio-economic or political structures. The Sherthukpens had to customarily purchase their essentials from the *haats* in the foothill bazaars of Assam until the 60s, when a township developed at Bomdila and revolutionised their lives, for better or worse, forever. They no longer had to make long hazardous journeys to procure necessary goods as the same could be had closer home, from the shiny new shops at Bomdila.

Every Sunday, Bomdila would play host to a motley band of folks who would trudge from across the glens and valleys in tow with their fowl, *jabrang*, eggs and chillies for the Sunday market in town. The people would take back home petty goods like salt, oil, soap and matchboxes in exchange of their articles. Roads served as the other major catalyst to change. The highway that ribbons up from Rupa to Bomdila and crosses the lofty Sela Pass connecting Tawang to the plains of Assam has been a lifeline to the people of the region. This artery of tar and concrete has paved the way for greater access and communication and considerably facilitated the economic life of the region.

In traditional tribal economy, slash and burn agriculture was the most significant mode of subsistence supplemented by gathering. The Sherthukpens were among the few tribes in the region that had traditionally developed terrace rice cultivation and used a primitive plough, entirely made of wood, which could only be used for soft soil. They were also one of the two tribes in Arunachal Pradesh to utilise the help of animals in farming.[1] Animals were also important for inter-tribal exchange. Forests not only provided food for the people but forest products were also common in trade and barter practices. Household goods, weapons, construction materials, water pipes, all were procured from the nearby woods. Hunting and fishing were also highly valued in the traditional economy. The local produce was enhanced by procuring rice from the Assam plains. Das (1995) writes, "Procurement of rice was one of the main objectives of the predatory raids of the villages in the plains by the hill tribes. During British rule, this mode of procurement changed from raid to trade."[2]

The pattern of land use, according to Das, graduated to an emergence of land ownership.

> They (Sherthukpens) were traditional jhumias till recently and had developed Adi-type (circular system) jhumming system besides their limited cultivation. A preliminary individual ownership of jhum land was recognised which enabled them to use, occupy and inherit the jhum plots. The right to dispose by means of sale was strictly prohibited. But an individual could hand over his jhum plots to others, if he desired so, in a particular jhum cycle. Village forests and fishing areas were demarcated for the use of different clans. Lands not occupied either by individuals or by clans were considered as common village land.[3]

The Sherthukpens continue to subsist mainly on agriculture; though *jhum* cultivation is gradually being replaced by settled cultivation. A section of the people are engaged in government service, working in various government departments as teachers, forest officers, guards, etc. There is no industry in the area and neither any industrial training for the people, with the exception of a government-run handicrafts and training centre at Bomdila. However, Sherthukpens are participants in the monetary economy and sell their produce of tomatoes, cabbage, maize and other vegetables and crops in the neighbouring markets. Some of the better-off Sherthukpens are also growing fruits and dry fruits like apples, strawberries, kiwis and walnuts.

A significant growth in the economic status of the people took place in the 70s, with the boom in the timber business. Many Sherthukpens, among other people living in the region, saw this as an opportunity to reap gold on zero investment. Large-scale unplanned felling of trees rendered many of the wooded forests and hills bare of life, consecutively exposing the people to the ethos that come with the market economy. The forests that had for generations provided to the people food and shelter were cut down mercilessly till eventually the timber trade was banned by the Supreme Court in 1996.

The most imposing site in Doimara, a village in the foothills amidst deep mysterious forests crawling with diverse animal and bird life, is the dilapidated remains of the Aiyo Sharmu Saw Mill. The mill, ironically named after the presiding deity of the adjoining forests, was the reason behind the establishment of Doimara as a permanent settlement. While the mill has perished, elephants roam freely, and both the village and the rare Great Indian Hornbill strive to thrive in the region. These dynamics could have been reversed had the mill been allowed to function.

The presence of money, in the present time, forms a fundamental economic basis in the lives of the Sherthukpens. However, it would not be incorrect to state that even today, many of the poor survive on the fringes of the monetary economy and continue to subsist on agricultural production, hunting and gathering activities. This may be substantiated by the simple fact that in the winter months, hunting is on an increase as agricultural produce is scarce. Many of the households in villages like Gorwa, Mukuthing and Membachur that are yet to be connected by a road, subsist on local resources and seldom visit the market at Rupa. Studying the consumption pattern of a number of households in the above-mentioned villages, in the months of January and February (2004), reveals that the people only use money to procure the most essential articles—matchboxes, oil, cloth, utensils, soap, salt. These are largely the same articles that were being purchased or bartered by their fathers and grandfathers. Money continues to be a scarce commodity and is only utilised for the most necessary requirements. This leads us to believe that the clan distinctions that prevailed traditionally and the economic pattern that emerged with the monetary system have largely benefited the elite while the poor remain marginalised. The introduction of the monetary economy has not managed to change the dynamics between the haves and the have-nots among the Sherthukpens. Das (1995) notes,

> Even after the introduction of panchayati raj in 1969, the structure of the village authorities has undergone little change. In most cases nobles of the old order have been rehabilitated in suitable position in the new hierarchy emerging under the new-socio-political order. This group of people having leadership qualities responded early towards the spread of modern education and new streams of economic activities. Because of their long habitual obedience, the commoners took a long time to respond to the changing socio-economic order. The educated class of elite, i.e. the tribal middle class in the State initially has emerged from the traditionally privileged section representing both continuity and change from their ancestors.[4]

Small-scale trading is another vital source of supplementary income. Crafts, animal products, vegetables and honey are important trading and exchange resources employed by the Sherthukpens. Some households also live on the economic returns from animal husbandry. However, wealth is no longer measured by the number of animals in a family but by the possession of mainstream material goods—car, *pucca* house, consumer goods, a government job and a sizable bank balance. Owing to the timber business, among others, many Sherthukpens especially in Rupa and Shergaon have plenty of the above.

Sherthukpens, especially those living in the semi-urban settlements, are increasingly earning their living through non-traditional methods like government jobs, running shops and working in organisations and offices in the state. The emergence of entrepreneurs, however, is a recent phenomenon as it was the Marwaris who have largely controlled trade and commerce not only in the Sherthukpen area but in much of Arunachal Pradesh. Das notes,

> The entire internal trade, i.e. the procurement of export items like rubber, cotton, long pepper, silk, etc. and the import of various manufactured goods were in the hands of the Marwari merchants right from the beginning of the British rule. Apart from trade in necessities, the Marwaris earned huge profit from opium and money-lending business.[5]

A number of shops in Rupa continue to be owned by the Marwaris. However, today some of the shops and other outlets like the snooker club in Rupa are being run by the locals.

AGRICULTURE

Farming remains the chief source of subsistence and the attachment of the people to their land forms the foundation of their security and well-being. Their skills, resources and specialist production still largely revolve around agriculture. Many of the well-to-do families reduce their workload by hiring servants and labourers to conduct their chores, which has enabled them to spare their children from agricultural activities and pursue education. Das observes,

> The rural rich has brought vast areas under permanent cultivation in order to establish the right of permanent possession over them. As a result, the size of the common village land has sharply been reduced leading to great hardship and deprivation of the co-villagers. The rising trend of concentration of cultivable land in the hands of a few and the emergence of agricultural labour in the Arunachal economy bear ample testimony to increasing vertical differentiation of the tribal communities of Arunachal... The process of accumulation in the hands of certain section of the local people has got a great fillip with the interlocking of economic and political powers.[6]

Slash and burn cultivation is still practised. The government has demarcated areas, based on the traditional patterns of land use that can be used by the people for the purpose. However, rampant clearing of forests has been checked under forest regulations. Clearing of reserved forests has been barred by the forest authorities. At present there is 675 hectares of land under cultivation in the Rupa Circle and the chief crops grown in the region are maize, soybean, finger millet, fox-tail millet, chilli, dry rice, French beans, kidney beans and barley.[7]

The poor Sherthukpen households in the villages and hamlets are mainly reliant on their family workforce and, on occasions, additional help from neighbours and clan members. After a long day of toil in the fields and forests, rest and respite come much like they did to their ancestors—with the simple joy of sipping *phak* before a crackling fire with friends and family.

TRADE AND BARTER

The Sherthukpens and Monpas could trade with Tibet as the ancient trade route to Tibet passes through the region inhabited by these tribes. This is believed to be the route that linked Assam to Tibet and once led to prosperous trade between them. Das notes,

> The Monpas, who until 1950 had been under Tibetan rule,[8] and the Sherthukpens also had played a long role of middlemen in trade between Assam and Tibet. While they used to go to Tibetan trading marts during the summer when the passes were open, they usually visited the Assam plains during the winter. Produces like chillies, vegetable dyes such as madder, peaches, handmade paper and husked rice were traded for Tibetan salt, wool and churpi (a hard cheese-like milk produce).[9]

Trade and barter practices with the Bhutanese were mainly limited to articles of Tibetan origin and Bhutanese trade was never prominent in the Arunachal frontier. However, the Bhutanese *tonga*, a coarse woollen cloth, is believed to have found favour with the people inhabiting the western borders of Arunachal. Reports also mention barter relations with the

Burmese people. However, these were mainly limited to the tribes inhabiting the eastern frontier of Arunachal. The Monpas and Sherthukpens supplied musk, blankets, cow tails, ponies, rock salt, swords, marijuana and different types of embroidered cloth and silk to the traders in Assam and purchased *lac*, silk, brass, copper, rice and other goods that were in demand in Tibet. The *haat* bazaars and trade fairs in the foothills went a long way in reorganising economic and non-economic exchanges between the Sherthukpens and the plains people. The fairs are said to have become more organised and were held at regular intervals since the late nineteenth century. The Sherthukpens mainly took back with them agricultural and simple products like rice, betel nut and leaf, cotton, tobacco, rape seed, thread, brass, copper and cloth. Transactions in such fairs could be made in both cash and kind. These fairs were largely replaced by weekly *haat* bazaars by the 1920s, which gradually paved the way for urban centres.

The Sherthukpens also traded with their other neighbours, namely the Monpas, Khowas, Akas and Mijis. The Sherthukpen masks, woven bags and knapsacks were extremely popular with their neighbours. These products were also traded with the Kacharis of the foothills.

MONEY-ORIENTED SYSTEM

It was the British who introduced money as the medium of exchange among the hill tribes. The British granted money in the form of an annual *posa* to prevent the hill tribes from raiding the plains and carrying away slaves. The tribals in Arunachal could also procure money in wages and remuneration or by performing other labour activities or by working as porters. But, while the elite were insured a regular supply of money from the rulers, the Chaos largely subsisted without money or a paltry amount of it. Some young men in the villages of Gorwa and Membachur informed me that they commonly earn money by working as day labourers in road building projects or by selling wood in towns during the winter months. "The rich need a crackling fire in their rooms even before they wake up," commented a young man.

NOTES AND REFERENCES

1. The other tribe to use animals in agricultural activities is said to be Khampti.
2. *Tribes of Arunachal Pradesh in Transition* by Gurudas Das (1995), pp. 26-27.
3. Ibid., p. 66.
4. *Tribes of Arunachal Pradesh in Transition* by Gurudas Das (1995), pp. 187-188.
5. *Tribes of Arunachal Pradesh in Transition* by Gurudas Das (1995), p. 189.
6. Ibid., p. 195.
7. The details have been obtained from Mr. S.C. Khrimey, APAS, Agriculture Development Officer, Rupa.
8. *Highlanders of Arunachal Pradesh* by Christoph von Fürer-Haimendorf (1982), p. 149. Das notes: It may be noted that the political status of Tawang inhabited by the Monpas was debatable. Initially, the British had the impression that the Monpas were of Tibetan origin, and since the ecclesiastical system of administration centring around the Tawang monastery was actually governed by its mother monastery, Drepung, in Tibet, they assumed Tawang to be a part of Tibet. Later, it was known that the Monpas came from Bhutan, not from Tibet and they expressed a preference for British rule, as opposed to the Tibetans. Perhaps that is why the Monpas accepted the McMohan Line ungrudgingly.
9. *Tribes of Arunachal Pradesh in Transition* by Gurudas Das (1995), p. 40.

5

Religion

> Religion itself has a history and, as such, it is a part of human history. The history of religion evolves, and this history is the story of the evolving human responses to the revelation of the divine. In short, religion itself evolves as mankind does. In this way, it transcends the idea that religion was an error—after all, if it is an error, Why does it continue to flourish? The creation of Hinduism antedates that of Buddhism. By this, I do not imply that Hinduism existed in India before Buddhism came into being—this claim, after all, is a standard textbook trivium—but that the Europeans created Buddhism after they had created Hinduism.[1]

The Sherthukpens simultaneously practise two distinct religions.

- Lamaism
- The Lo religion, or the worship of Khik[2]

Investigations on the Sherthukpen religions are rendered somewhat difficult and hard to grasp as the Sherthukpens combine the two religions—Lamaism and the Lo religion (or the 'Worship of Khik')—distinctly in different areas. Over a period of time the two religions have also acquired and borrowed from each other, thereby making it difficult to decipher with certainty the origin of the prevalent religious practices.

The situation is further complicated as the source of the Lamaist teachings introduced in the region is not known. The faith could be an import from Bhutan or Tibet. Also, there is an evident admixture of the unreformed

Nyingmapa, the old sect which amalgamated many customs originating from the Bon as its religious practices. In addition, the neighbouring Monpa tribe could have had considerable influence on the Sherthukpens, which perhaps led them to adopt the faith as well. The Monpas are believed to have been under the sway of Lamaism from the 11th century or according to another theory from 8th century, and continue to practise some pre-Lamaist Bon as well as indigenous traditions till this day.

The Lo religion may be described as an animist-shamanist faith that delves in the belief of both good and evil powers. The Lo has a number of deities, gods and goddesses; the spirits dwelling in the surrounding mountains of the Sherthukpen territory acquire the most significant place in the religious system. The chief practitioner of this faith is the *dzizi* who acts as a mediator between the spirits and the people.

Broadly, the Sherthukpens of Rupa practise both Lamaism and the Lo religion but a visible split may be discerned between the two schools of faith. This split, however, is not as evident in the religious practices of Shergaon, where both the Lama and *dziz* seem to coexist in relative harmony. The Sherthukpens of some of the far-flung villages or *pams*, on the other hand, have little to do with Lamaism in their everyday life. Indeed, many of the people there may never summon a Lama throughout their lifetime, but it is on the occasion of death that the Lamaist rites and rituals must be observed. Judging by the prevalent practices in the hamlets or *busties* and the available information and investigations on the religious histories of Rupa and Shergaon, it might be indicated that Lamaism is a relatively recent introduction to the mainstream religion of the Sherthukpens although there is evidence to show that it has existed on the sidelines from earlier times.

Haimendorf writes,

> All Sherdukpens consider themselves as Buddhists and in Rupa there is a large and well appointed Nyingmapa gompa in which the usual Buddhist rites are performed. But the three Lamas in charge have come from Bhutan, and in 1980 there was no Sherdukpen training as Lama in any of the gompas of Kameng District. When a *Wang* rite is to be performed Lamas from Dirang

of Tawang are invited, and today Lamas from the Tibetan refugee settlement of Tenjigaon are also available for such celebrations. Buddhism appears to be of relatively recent introduction, and an older indigenous religion centering around the worship of *Khik* seems to be much more deeply rooted in the Sherdukpen tradition.[3]

The above observation was made by the anthropologist based on his fieldwork conducted around 1980. However, today, 24 years later, it might be said that Lamaism has acquired greater prominence among the people in the semi-urban settlements of Rupa and Shergaon as well as in the *busties* immediately neighbouring the two, whereas the Sherthukpens of the secluded villages and hamlets predominantly continue to prescribe to their indigenous faith or the Lo.

Minister of State D.K. Thondok, a Sherthukpen from Rupa, is currently writing an account on the Sherthukpen ancestors and is of the belief that Lamaism was introduced to the Sherthukpens as early as AD 1500. His research (mainly based on his readings of the *Pechha*[4]) reveals that Lamaism was brought to the Sherthukpens by Lama Trampie Dreama, who, according to him, was a student of the second Dalai Lama. Correspondingly, J.N. Chowdhury notes that the founding of the Tawang monastery and Lamaism among the Monpas is associated with Lama Mera, "reported to have lived in the time of the 5th Dalai Lama of Tibet".[5] However, it seems unlikely that the Sherthukpens began to practise Lamaism before the Monpas, as the religion seems to be much more deeply embedded in the Monpa culture, as compared to that of the Sherthukpens.

In the opinion of Haimendorf, Lamaism was an influence of the Tibetan, Monpa or Bhutanese Lamas on the Sherthukpens. He writes, "The establishment of Buddhist institutions may be due to the impact of more recent activity of Tibetan, Bhutanese of Monpa Lamas."[6]

LAMAISM

According to Haimendorf, the origins of Lamaism in western Arunachal Pradesh can be traced back to the 11th century.

He writes,

> The great majority of the tribal societies of Arunachal Pradesh share a world view and a social atmosphere that have remained outside the orbit of the great historic civilisations of South Asia. Despite the spatial proximity of Assam on one side, and of Tibet on the other, neither Hinduism nor Buddhism impinged on these societies, most of which persisted until recently in a state of isolation from extraneous influences. However, there is one part of Arunachal Pradesh where for several centuries very different conditions prevailed and tribal societies evince the powerful cultural impact of Mahayana Buddhism in its Lamaistic form. This region, which adjoins to the west the mountain kingdom of Bhutan, differs from the rest of Arunachal Pradesh both topographically and culturally. Whereas elsewhere the nature of the terrain had prevented the development of caravan routes suitable for pack-animals, in the westernmost part of Arunachal Pradesh there are climatic and geographical conditions which favoured the opening of trade routes linking the territory both with Tibet and the plains of Assam. Hence, conditions were similar to those prevailing in Bhutan and further west in Sikkim and Nepal. Along these trans-Himalayan trade routes Tibetan cultural elements and ultimately Buddhist monks and nuns infiltrated into the mountain region lying between the easternmost part of Bhutan and the southern border of Tibet. As a result of these cultural and ethnic influences from the north, the region, now dominated by the famous monastery of Tawang, assumed a character entirely different from that of the (other) parts of Arunachal Pradesh.[7]

The form of Buddhism dominantly practised in the Himalayan belt is termed as Lamaism and not Buddhism by most scholars, as the faith stems from Mahayana Buddhism and not Hinayana or Vajrayana. The prevalent religion originates mainly from the Mahayana school of Buddhism combined with Tantric Hindusim, some Mongolian elements and the Tibetan Bon religion—pre-Buddhist faith of Tibet. This branch of Buddhism has often been considered inferior, and referred to as mere 'priest-craft'. In addition, this branch of Lamaism has been considered as "un-Buddhistic" by scholars like L.A. Wadell (1934).

The key traits of Lamaism may be described thus:

> Priesthood and sanctity are acquired by learning and not by inspiration; the sacrifice of animals is a heinous sin; the future

> can be learned by calculations from the holy books and not by inspiration; the soul of the dead wanders for a short time in a sort of purgatory, before being reincarnated either in another form on this earth, or going to some heaven or hell, as different as imagination can make them from anything experienced on earth. Most important of all, Lamaism's ethics are founded on a belief in individual destiny and a sense of sin. Lamaism contains a long, explicit and detailed list of sins which can be committed by human beings, and which have repercussions on the evil-doer, first by feelings of remorse and then by punishment either in this life or in future reincarnations.[8]

Apparently, the first people in Arunachal Pradesh to adopt Lamaism were the Monpas who are mainly concentrated in the districts of West Kameng and Tawang. Going by the belief that the Sherthukpens have adopted Lamaism only at a later date, it may be assumed that they were deeply influenced by their Monpa and Bhutanese neighbours and the organised and grand nature of their religion which perhaps gradually inspired the Sherthukpens to adopt Lamaism.

Haimendorf writes,

> According to local tradition, the Tawang valley came under Buddhist influence as early as the 11th century, when a monk from the Bumtang district of Bhutan established several villages of adherents of the new faith. The first monasteries in the area were foundations of the Kargyupa and Nyingmapa sects, and it is believed that in the 13th century the Drukpa branch of the Kargyupa sect was introduced by another monk from Bhutan. Later, when the Gelugpa sect had attained a dominant position in Tibet, Lodre Gyatso, a Lama from the Tibetan village of Meram and hence popularly known as Mera Lama, set out to spread the Gelugpa doctrine among the Monpas of Tawang and succeeded in this endeavour with the help of the fifth Dalai Lama (1617–1682). It was during this period that the foundations of the great Gelugpa monastery of Tawang were laid.[9]

Sarkar writes,

> The Lamas and the laity firmly believe that Lopon Rimpoche visited the Monpa as well as Sherdukpen areas and planted the germ of Buddhism there... Lopon Rimpoche and Lopon Pema Jungne are the local names of Padmasambhava.[10] The legends, therefore, place the visit of the Master, if not the advent of Buddhism itself, in the eighth century.[11]

> ...The tradition about the eighth century visit of Padmasambhava to the area occupied presently by the Sherthukpens provides no clue to the actual date of their conversion to Buddhism. Some booklets in the Tawang monastery mention that Meme Gyapten (Japtang Bura), whom the Sherthukpens honour as their ancestor, came to this area as a lay associate of Tanpie Dronme sometime between 1475 and 1543. Kechang Doyen Tanjing, the sixth incarnation of Tranpie Dronme, established Buddhism among them some time around 1742.[12]

Sarkar reveals that three 'Buddhist' sects, namely Nyingmapa, Kargyupa and Gelugpa operated in Western Arunachal Pradesh. Gelugpa was the last sect to come to this area and it firmly established itself in the region over time. The Karmapa, a sub-sect of the Kargyupa, was eradicated completely. The Nyingmapa lingers on but it is mainly practised by village priests.

> The Nyingmapa has three sub-sects here, namely, Tresar, Konchochindu and Peling. The Sherdukpens have only the Tresar. The difference between these sub-sects is that they have different revelations or terma treatises as the code of demonical worship. These terma works are held to have been written by Padmasambhava....[13]

Chattopadhyay, in his *Lepchas and their Heritage*, outlines the journey of Lamaism into the eastern belt of Indian Himalayas and also gives a brief, though critical, history of Buddhism and Tibetan Buddhism or Lamaism.

> Lamaism is essentially priestcraft and an impure form of Buddhism that was introduced in Tibet in the middle of the seventh century. It owed its origin to tantrism supposed to have been propagated by Arya Asanga, a Buddhist monk of Peshawar, who lived about 300 AD... It (Buddhism) was the earliest organised religion with the quickest spread (later, Christianity and Mohammedanism have dimmed its record) and four great councils were held in different areas and climes to regulate its missionary growth. The fourth council at Jalandhar in Punjab held under the aegis of King Kanishka (1st century AD) of Kashmir and Punjab witnessed a schism over the polemic of exorcism

between the 'northern' and the 'southern school' advocating the more primitive and purer form with Pali as the medium. The 'northern school' incorporated bolder concepts of a progression of several grades of theoretical Buddhas and of numerous divine Budhisatwas.... When 'northern' Buddhism found its way to Tibet through the good officers of Sron-tsan Gampo's Chinese wife, it had already gathered dregs of impurity.... Nevertheless, tantrism was not so much of a force then in Tibet than a hundred years later, when Padmasambhava came to this country at the request of King Khri-Sron-De-Tsan (AD 755–797). He introduced tantric Buddhism in Tibet which held a steady sway for about decadence. It was at this critical juncture in AD 1042 that Chandragarbh @ Atish (982–1054) visited Tibet from Vikramashila Buddhist University in Bihar... Chandragarbha travelled far and wide including Sumatra and rare to fame as the brightest luminary of the Buddhist lore. He was no believer in magic but preached celibacy, moral abstinence and shunning of the practice of magic... He took a synthetic view of the 'Mahayana' and 'Hinayana' traditions of Buddhism and established monastic discipline among Tibetans, bringing the majority of them under its influence. The reformed sect was called the Kah-dam-pa or 'those bound by orders'. Three and a half centuries later, in another reformer Tsong-kha-pa's hands the order became more ritualistic and less ascetic and became known as Ge-lugs-pa or 'Yellow Hats' – the most dominant sect in Tibet... Incidentally, Ge-lugs-pa later found favour with Mongolian rulers and Altan Khan, King of Thumed Mongolia as the first veritable Dalai ("Ocean"). The conferment of sovereignty of the whole of Tibet on the fifth Dalai Lama (1615–1680) by the Mongolian chief Gusri Khan was only a predictable follow-up. Those who continued to subscribe to the old tantric beliefs and mode of dressing and refused to be reformed came to be known as Rnin-m-pa; or 'Red Hats.'

... as soon as the news of his (Buddha's) death (May, 544 BC) spread, a section of monks like Subhadra became jubilant and thought that this was the end of the tyranny of the monastic order... within a hundred years, the Master's final foreboding came true and dissension arose with regard to his actual words

> and their interpretations. In a couple of hundred years, eighteen or more sects came into existence. But all his intellectual power would have found it difficult to conceive a phenomenon like the Lama of the Tibetan variety, who is content to look at the world through his inscrutable laden eyes, having drugs or sex on the sly and turn the meditative time-wheel with monotonous precision. The absence of contemplative or intellectual element in practical Lamaism is dangerous, because this will eventually make all rituals, arts, moral legislation and the 'active life' in general fall apart through lack of principle to unify them. Today a Lama is made, not born, and priest-craft is learnt and sanctity acquired by constant practice and not by inspiration. At least this dictum applies to the ordinary Lamahood, while the higher posts may need vicarious traits and considerations, sometimes looking beyond regional boundaries.[14]

The Lamas in the Rupa Monastery that follows the Nyingmapa sect admit that Lamahood attracts few aspirants. Even today, there are no Sherthukpen Lamas admitted to the Rupa Gompa. Lama Yeshi Tenzing, the head Lama of the Rupa monastery aged 34, and a Bhutanese who came to India in 1976, mentioned that out of the 24 Lamas in the monastery, none were Sherthukpen and most of the admitted Lamas were either orphans or boys from poor families. He stated that Gelukpa and Nyingmapa sects are both different branches of the same school of thought, but according to him the chief distinction between the existing Gelukpa and Nyingmapa sects are as follows: As opposed to Gelukpa, the Nyingmapa sect is a more prominent branch of the Vajrayana School, which embodies a greater spiritual inclination and emphasis on meditation. Lama Yeshi Tenzing said that true practitioners of Nyingmapa could even predict the time of their death and are believed to abandon their bodies with great ease. He said that great powers are bestowed on married Lamas, as they can practise an extremely powerful and esoteric form of yoga that is only performed with a partner of the opposite sex. The Lama added that he had practised the yoga for a period of one year in Bhutan, about 13 years ago, at the Parotaksang Ashram. Father of three children, Lama Yeshi Tenzing admitted that he had never practised the yoga with his wife.

The Lama stated that eating meat was not considered pious but if a Lama should consume meat, he must read some mantras to salvage the spirit of the dead beast. He admitted to eating beef until he gave it up about two years ago, but said that he had only consumed cows killed by accident. According to him, 80% of the Lamas in Rupa were vegetarian and 100% were teetotallers. This claim, however, was refuted by many locals in Rupa who have personally witnessed a number of Lamas consuming meat as well as alcohol. I was also informed that Lama Yeshi Lepcha himself gave up eating beef primarily because of some medical complications after which the doctor had advised him to give up eating beef.

Dziz Tshering Norbu Dingla, aged 82, says the Lamas came to Rupa when he was 46 years old. According to Lama Yeshi Tenzing, Lamaism came to Rupa about 200 years ago. It is, however, unclear as to whether the Sherthukpens are originally followers of the Gelukpa or the Nyingmapa sect. The aforementioned Minister of State, D.K. Thondok, is of the belief that Sherthukpens are Gelukpa followers as Lamaism was brought to the Sherthukpens around AD 1500 by Lama Tanpie Dronme, a student of the Dalai Lama.[15] But he was unclear as to how the Rupa monastery came to belong to the Nyingmapa, instead of the Gelukpa sect. However, it is known from the histories of Tibet and Bhutan that clartes for deminion between the Bhutanese Dukpas and Monpa Gelugpas started in 1643. The Mongol-Tibetan troops also assisted the Monpas against the Bhutanese army in 1647, following which the Tawang monastery was established in the same year.[16]

Two queries arise from the above observations. The first is the period of introduction of Lamaism in the Sherthukpen society, and the second, the uncertainty of whether the Sherthukpens are originally, and now, followers of the Gelukpa or Nyingmapa sect.

Going by the above claims, establishing the accurate time frame of the adoption of Lamaism by the Sherthukpens is clearly not a straightforward task. The near absence of authoritative work on the Sherthukpens also makes the task of exploration not a simple one. Nevertheless, it could be said that even in the case of Rupa—the stronghold of Lamaism in the Sherthukpen territory—last rites of most of their grandparents were performed by Lamas.

The establishment of the Nyingmapa order at the monastery in Rupa could be a result of its proximity to Bhutan as the Nyingmapa was widespread in Bhutan. It could be supposed that Nyingmapa Lamas came to dominate the religious life there and established the Nyingmapa monastery. Even today, the most important Lama in Rupa is Bhutanese. However, there is no evidence to suggest that the Nyingmapa Lamas might have replaced an earlier dominant Gelukpa presence. Sarkar notes,

> He (Kechang Doyen Tanjing) also visited the Sherthukpen area, where he established Buddhism in and Shergaon were built when the people took to the Buddhist faith. The Rupa Gonpa was constructed in 1742 according to the record preserved there. Kechang Doyen Tanjing went back to Ehlageri (Tibet) where he died.[17]

It must be pointed out that according to the residents of Rupa, the edifice that is today known as the Rupa gompa was earlier a fort where the Sherthukpens would collect to fight and ward off hostile attacks from the neighbouring tribes. Hence, the above reference does not clarify the existing confusion. The Rupa monastery predates the coming of Lamaism to Rupa. Constructed perhaps in 1742 as stated above, or 1672 (though some claim that the gompa was constructed in 1525), the gompa was originally the Lomed Fort where the people of the village took refuge when attacked by the warring Akas.

Investigation in the period of transformation of the dominant religion of the Sherthukpens today is not straightforward as the Sherthukpens combine the two religions—Lamaism and the Lo—distinctly in different areas. The Sherthukpens of Rupa practise both Lamaism and the Lo but a visible split can be detected between the two schools of faith. The split, however, is not as evident in the region of Shergaon where both the Lama and *dzizi* (indigenous Sherthukpens priests) seem to coexist in great harmony. The chief rationale behind this dichotomy is perhaps that while most of the prominent Lamas in the Rupa gompa come from Bhutan, the ones in the monastery at Shergaon are locals and thus familiar with and sensitive to the local belief system. The Sherthukpens of *busties* like Gorwa and Dingla seem to exhibit some suspicion and distrust over the Bhutanese Lamas in Rupa. And even though the monastery in Rupa is nearest to them, they prefer to summon Lamas from elsewhere. The Bhutanese monks, on the other hand, consider the Lo religion somewhat pagan and are gradually trying to obliterate it from the active imagination of the people. This is evident from the words of Lama Yeshi Tenzing who said, "In another 25-30 years people will stop believing in the *dzizi*." He elaborated, "My impression of the *dzizi* is that he mainly concentrates on ghosts and evil spirits." Commenting on the evolving change among the people of Rupa, he said, "People will gradually leave the path of the *dzizi* as this passage is not for the good. We try to explain to the people that following the *dzizi* is a '*paap*' or misdeed."

Recounting the changes brought about by Lamaism in the region the Lama said,

> I have been in Rupa for 24 years. No one has said that he will not give up the *dzizi*. The intensity of faith in the *dzizis* has decreased dramatically in my years in Rupa. It has come down from 100% to 30%. Violence has come down as well. Earlier the people would constantly talk ill about each other, they were also very jealous of those more fortunate than them. Buddhism has changed this and now the people are calmer. Alcoholism too has come down from 100% to 25%.

The Sherthukpens in Rupa do not agree with the assessment of the Lama. Instead, many are of the opinion that people were more god-fearing and less materialistic a few decades ago. However, most people admit that Lama Yeshi Tenzing's opinion on alcoholism is accurate. Even so, this is perhaps more an impact of education and awareness rather than religion.

The divide between the Lo and Lamaism does not seem to be so pronounced in Shergaon. *Dzizi* Tanla Thungon, aged 74, also the seniormost *Gaonburah* of Shergaon, is of the opinion that the Lo religion has not faced a setback because of Lamaism. "We are Buddhists and Lama puja was done in every family since I was a little boy and even before I was born. I do not believe that the Lamas are trying to discourage the *dzizi*. In fact, Lamas still call the *dzizi* when they fall ill." The Lamas in Shergaon are locals and most of them are either from Shergaon or from the surrounding hamlets and villages. A curious feature of the religious practices of Shergaon is that the most important Lo ceremony or the annual Khiksaba at Shergaon is conducted by a Lama.[18] Hence, it would not be out of line to say that the two religions have combined and evolved differently in different Sherthukpen territories.

The Sherthukpens of some of the far-flung villages or *busties*, on the other hand, have little to do with Lamaism in their everyday life. Indeed, many of the people here may never summon a Lama throughout their lifetime, but it is on the occasion of death that the Lamaist rites and rituals must be observed. The presence of the *dzizi* is central to the well-being of these *busti* dwellers. The Sherthukpens dwelling in these hamlets feel that while they could do without the Lama, life without the *dzizi* in the village scenario is unimaginable. They also concede that Lamas are mainly for the rich people in the semi-urban settlements of Rupa and Shergaon. This opinion could be of some merit, as calling a Lama is certainly not a simple or an inexpensive venture. Firstly, there are no Lamas living in these distant villages, and in order to summon them, people have to walk the distance to the nearest monastery in the towns. The village Gorwa has been recently connected by an unpaved path to Rupa. But so far, there is no public transport service that links these villages and in spite of the new path, the villagers continue to walk to the town for their chores. I was told by the villagers that the Lamas come to the *busties* in cars and jeeps and do not walk like the locals. Moreover, unlike the *dzizi* who is given anything from foodgrains to a few rupees for his services, the Lama has to be treated as a revered guest, served with an elaborate meal and presented with at least a few hundred rupees. This is clearly out of reach of most *busti* dwellers. To a certain extent, this sentiment also prevails among the poorer Sherthukpens in Rupa. The most common reason for not actively practising 'Buddhism' given was '*hum nahin kar sakega*' or 'we cannot afford the Lama'.

When you ask a Sherthukpen about what religion he follows, the singular answer will be 'Buddhism'. I did not come across a single person even in the remote hamlets who gave a different answer. Such is the sway of Lamaism in the region that the average Sherthukpen or Monpa has acquired a condescending attitude towards the non-Lamaist tribes of Arunachal Pradesh. I was often told that the Adis, Akas and Mijis do not have any dharma. *'Unka koi dharm nahin hai.'* This is said in spite of the common knowledge that the mentioned tribes are sun-moon worshippers. The opinion of *dzizi* Tshering Norbu Diingla on his religion was revealing. When asked what his religion was, he answered, "Buddhism." But on probing further, he revealed that he had never called a Lama to his home. "I call myself Buddhist because the whole village calls itself Buddhist. But I do not pray to any Buddhist god or Lama. My gods are the spirits of the Lo." I was also told by some school children that before their exams begin, they can never think of praying to the Buddha or Dalai Lama. The only one who automatically comes to their mind is their local *dzizi*. Interestingly, many other villagers also reported the same. In moments of crisis and need, Sherthukpens predominantly think of their *dzizi* even in Rupa. I only came across a couple of people who said the contrary. The people in question were deeply religious and were told by the Bhutanese Lama that in order to follow 'Buddhism' they had to abandon their old belief system. Namgey Wangmu Thongon, aged 63, of Rupa, said that she had left the path of the Lo because it involved animal sacrifice. She also said that the last time she had called the *dzizi* to her house was over four years back. The *dzizi* was called to perform the Soksing ritual, which is observed for the long life and well being of an individual. She said, "Abu, my youngest son, was leaving for Maharashtra to pursue engineering so I had to perform the Shoksing pooja." However, in the past four years Namgey Wangmu Thongon has become a more serious follower of the Lamaist faith and says that she will be unable to call the *dzizi* to perform the ritual for her daughter, presently appearing for Class 12 board exams, if she wishes to study outside like her brother. It can be concluded from the above that the adoption of Lamaism within the mainstream religion of the Sherthukpens is not immensely old.

This, more than any other observation, reflects that Lamaism has indeed not had a deep impact on much of the Sherthukpen psyche as yet, and that the sway of the Lo is still considerable, though not as esteemed or fashionable. This is true even though symbols of Lamaism dominate the Sherthukpen territory. Every sizable town and village has a monastery or at least a makeshift structure that serves as a monastery. Dongzurs, chortens, maneys[19] and prayer flags can be spotted in every habitable direction and a string of prayer flags is suspended above almost every Sherthukpen house. A number of homes even have elaborate Lamaist alters that support intricate statues and portraits of Buddhist deities and sacred books. An extremely elaborate monastery is presently being constructed at Chillipam (about 8,200 ft), a village located on one of the highest hills circling the valley of Rupa. This monastery boasts intricate workmanship and borrows heavily from Bhutanese architecture and craft. Artisans and craftsmen have been called in from Bhutan and Nepal to work on the edifice. Residents of Rupa and the surrounding *busties* have given generous donations for the monastery that promises to be a prominent tourist attraction and are following its progress with avid zeal.

THE LO RELIGION OR THE WORSHIP OF KHIK

I have chosen to term the indigenous faith of the Sherthukpens as the Lo religion (even though most Sherthukpens themselves are not familiar with the term) because it was described as "the name of all the Sherthukpen gods and goddesses put together," by Tshering Norbu Dingla, of Rupa, arguably the most powerful and senior Sherthukpen *dzizi*, or priest. I have not come across any other reference to the term Lo, and from my knowledge, no scholar has so far investigated the religion in any detail although some anthropologists and survey officers have mentioned that the Sherthukpens practise an animist local faith. Haimendorf calls the faith the 'Worship of Khik' but does not explore the religion further, mainly concentrating on the neighbouring and more populous Monpa tribe. Perhaps Haimendorf adopted the term 'Khik' from the biggest indigenous festival of the Sherthukpens called the Khiksaba. However, the 'Worship of Khik' is an important annual rite practised for the general well-being of the people and cannot be used as an apt term to address the religion. Khik is merely another name for the most powerful Lo deity commonly known as Sunkhik, who is invoked during the festival. The term Lo, on the other hand, embodies the power of all the Lo supernaturals and is thus aptly representative of the faith. The term Lo shall be used in the report to address the indigenous religion of the Sherthukpens.

R.R.P. Sharma has attempted a description of the religion; however, he does not probe the fundamental nature of the faith itself. He writes,

> The Sherdukpen religion is a curious blend of Buddhism and local beliefs. The people venerate the Buddhist spiritual leaders and worship in the Gompas which have images of Lord Buddha and his disciples. They also have a good deal of faith in their own local deities and spirits whose help they invariably invoke in times of distress and suffering.[20]

The Lo religion may be described as an animist-shamanist faith that delves in the belief of both good and evil powers. Its chief function is to help people cope with misfortune and offer release from suffering, as well as achieve or enhance prosperity, healing, divination and control. The system of faith holds that misfortune is the result of evil or enraged spirits that may be tempered with ceremonies of exorcism or propitiation. Gauging from the past and prevalent trends, it can be said that the primary function of the religion is more utilitarian than sublime. Nonetheless, elements of a spiritual quest are not altogether absent in its practice and beliefs.

The origin of the Lo is impossible to decipher today but it can be said with certainty that the faith has been with the Sherthukpens since ancient times and predates the adoption of Lamaism.

The religion has a number of gods and goddesses who the Sherthukpens worshipped at regular intervals to evade their wrath and the resulting misfortune. Unlike Lamaism, the Lo religion does not have a strict social organisation. The chief practitioners of this faith are called the *dzizis* who act as mediators between the spirits and people. Spirits dwelling in the surrounding mountains of the Sherthukpen territory acquire the most significant place in the religious system. Forests, rivers, rocks and other natural objects are also believed to be the abode of the supernatural. All catastrophes are said to be caused by spirits and thus the spirits need to be propitiated with mandatory sacrifice and rituals. Ceremonies and rituals are central to the faith and are performed to secure a protected and healthy life as well as relief from misfortune. The Sherthukpens also perform purification and fertility rites.

The facet of the supernatural and people's accountability to it is predominant, and ceremonies and rituals engender a peaceful relationship between man and the elements. Rituals create a given worldview, brace the worth of institutional structure and reinforce social relationships. Rituals are also important social events and serve as a meeting ground for people who gather in large numbers to eat, drink and socialise on religious occasion. Rites also function as important social and cultural events offering respite from the monotony of day-to-day existence. Rituals sanction large-scale meetings and revelry as well as endeavour to reinstate normacy in times of hardship.

Comparison between Lamas and the Lo Priests or *Dzizis*

Lamaistic practices with elements of occult, tantra and the propitiation of spirits via chanting and rituals were also the common features of the Lo religion. Thus, the adoption of Lamaism by the Sherthukpens was not necessarily dramatic. Instead, the inclusion of Lamaism, has been a gradual process which continues in the present times. Lama Yeshi Tenzing said, "A *dzizi* can find only temporary cure to relieve people who are possessed by spirits, whereas we Lamas can release the troubled spirit eternally." However, unlike Lamaism, the Lo religion does not have any strict social organisation. The *dzizis*, by the virtue of being possessed by a supernatural, have certain gifts and duties, but their status is not enhanced by any title.

Nevertheless, they do command certain esteem in society which is not formalised. Sango Wangmo, the wife of *Dzizi* Tshering Norbu Dingla, says, "I was happy to be married to a *dzizi* because everyone used to respect them. I was proud of my husband as he was a priest, doctor, healer and so many other things put together." It might also be of significance to point out that this respect for the *dzizi* was never demonstrated as it is in the case of Lamas. The *dzizi* was, and is, considered 'one of them and their own', whereas the same affinity is not shared with the Lamas.

Unlike Lamas, the *dzizis* do not have any special dress distinguishing them from the average Sherthukpen. In addition to this, no special ceremony takes place when a *dzizi* dies, as the spirit that had possessed the priest is believed to have no concern with the soul of the dead. There is also no divinisation attached to a *dzizi* after his death as is the case, say, among the nomads of northern Siberia, where the shaman is part of a more complex society and after death, he may be the object of a regular cult as the shaman is transformed into a god. In rare cases, these elements also exist in Lamaism.

Another disparity between the two religions is the status of their female priests. Female Lamas or in-e-bu are subordinate to Lamas and are not allowed to conduct ceremonies or perform exorcism at par with the Lamas. However, in the Sherthukpen pantheon, women do not seem to occupy a less important place than men do. I did not come across any female *dzizi* but was informed by *dzizi* Tshering Norbu Dingla that he had known of two female *dzizis* from Shergaon who were as powerful as the male *dzizis*. However, Sherthukpen female priests are rare and, by and large, the *dzizi* is male.

The Lo Deities

Given the nature of the Sherthukpen territory, predictably, the most important supernatural element in the Lo is believed to be the spirits of the mountains. These mountains tower over the Sherthukpen belt and engender forests that offer to the people ingredients of their basic livelihood—wood to build their homes and other utilitarian goods, while flora and fauna constituted the daily diet.

The important deities of the Sherthukpen Lo religion are the following:

Synkhik – Mountain god, also the most important Lo deity

Soro – Mountain god, close to the *busti* Brokpu Blong

Nambo – Mountain god close to the *busti* Thungri

Ngamphu – Mountain god close to Shergaon

Zdingkho – River spirit by Rupa

Neabong – Mountain god close to Rupa, now taken over by the army

Jhumoropki – Mountain god beyond Rupa

Jhumowongktsi – Mountain god close to Shergaon

Sakar Dema – Mountain spirit close to Shergaon

Lablong, Chankon and Jamu – Tree spirits of Rupa

The older *dzizis* say that there were some legends associated with these spirits but they could not recollect them in any detail. This reflects a change in the general attitude of the Sherthukpens towards their indigenous faith.

The Lo Priests

The *dzizi* is the main priest of the Sherthukpens and has many similarities with other tribal priests across the Himalayan belt. The *dzizi* is believed to be empowered to avert and impede the influence of harmful spirits, appease the good spirits, cure illnesses, and mollify the spirits to grant general well-being. In ancient times, they performed all the rituals dealing with important events of the life of the Sherthukpens and presided over important ceremonies, festivals and marriages. The *dzizi* performs ceremonies for the individual, his household and for a geographical group of households or the *busti* or *busties*.

The role of the *dzizi* is usually inherited within the family. However, it is not always restricted to the particular family line and exceptions are known to occur. In addition, the spirit does not necessarily manifest itself in every generation. Anyone can become a *dzizi* provided he or she acquires the necessary supernatural powers. However, *dzizis* are usually from the Dingla clan who are among the Chaos and, therefore, lower in status than the Thongs. The clan restriction of a *dzizi* is a curiously interesting aspect of the Lo and perhaps throws some light on the system of clan hierarchy of the Sherthukpens. These aspects shall be examined further in the report.[21]

The process of picking a *dzizi* is akin to that of many other tribal religions of the world and is determined by symptoms of mental depression, delirium and illness. However, the *dzizi* experiences some eating aversions which are unique to the Lo. The *dzizi* is believed to have a strong repugnance to eating garlic, onion and meat. This aversion is believed to be so strong that people have to clean their homes of all these articles when they summon a *dzizi*. Over a period, these symptoms are observed by the people, supernatural intervention is gradually confirmed and the person in question is accepted as a *dzizi*. However, no formal events mark the advent of a new *dzizi* in the Sherthukpen society.

Dzizi Tshering Norbu Dingla of Rupa, 82, claims that he was possessed by the spirit when he was 15 years old. He believes that his possession was fated and describes the period of his initiation as a powerful one. He says, "The spirit that came to me was the power of the mountains combined with the spirit of my father who was also a *dzizi*." He describes the symptoms as a combination of madness, delirium and a feeling of possessing special powers. He adds, "If anyone came into my house, I would start throwing everything outside, bite myself and behave like a madman. After some time my family realised that this was no ordinary event and they promptly lit some incense and cleaned the house. This calmed me considerably."

The *dzizi* does not undergo any formal training but receives instruction through the medium of dreams. Norbu Dingla says, "Gradually I started dreaming about some of the older *dzizis* who had passed away and they started to coach me in the esoteric knowledge." *Dzizi* Tangla Thungon, of Shergaon, says,

> My *devtas* come to me in my dreams and that is how I am continuously taught and instructed. I see a female spirit in my sleep. She is dressed in a suit of iron and also wears a metal cap and shoes and carries a gun and *dao* (local knife in a wooden scabbard traditionally carried by Sherthukpen men). She tells me what to do and even predicts some events, and commands me to perform my duties properly. She keeps a constant check

on me. I am familiar with her power and am scared to stray from my path and experience her wrath.

The *dzizi* also said that he dreams of a less imposing male *devta* who assists and teaches him regularly.

There is no criterion of age to become a *dzizi* but once an individual is declared a *dzizi,* he has to practise a number of taboos. The most important set of restrictions on a *dzizi* are imposed on his diet. After attainment of dzizihood, a priest cannot eat garlic, onion, eggs and the flesh of domesticated animals. However, he is allowed to eat the flesh of certain wild animals and also some varieties of small fish. In my observations, these taboos seem to be somewhat flexible and tend to change from village to village. There are no restrictions on the sexual or social life of a *dzizi*.

STATUS AND CHANGE

"Earlier I was the proud wife of the *dzizi* who people respected. Today when he goes to distant places at late hours, I sit and worry about him because people do not take care of him like they used to."

Sango Wangmo, wife of *Dzizi* Tshering Norbu Dingla, Age – 80, Rupa.

Evaluating the present status of the *dzizi* and the existing impact of the Lo religion is a multi-tiered process. Different areas of the Sherthukpen belt exhibit different indications. As mentioned above, the Lo religion seems to have the least impact in Lama-dominant Rupa, whereas Shergaon, the other semi-urban settlement, does not reveal the same lack of impact of the Lo. In the remote Sherthukpen villages, however, Lamaism has not yet penetrated or replaced the Lo, and the local faith continues to be the mainstream religion here. This is not to say that Lamaism is the chief cause of the extinction of the Lo, but, what might be said is that Lamaism is gradually replacing the Lo in areas like Rupa where the hold of the indigenous faith seems to be weakening. Another interesting observation that can be made here is that the replacement of the Lo by Lamaism is most prominent in the most developed areas and the least in the pockets that remain remote and underdeveloped. Perhaps this brings to conclude that not only has the advent of Lamaism put the Lo in the sidelines but also that modernity and development have played a significant part in sidelining the Lo faith.

Today, with the coming of the Lamas, the esteem of the *dzizi* has diminished considerably and so has the extent and influence of their functions. *Dzizi* Tshering Norbu Dingla says,

> The Lamas came to Rupa when I was 46. The Lamas were not very important in my younger days. Perhaps because when the Lamas were called for a puja the result would only show after one year while a puja conducted by a *dzizi* shows instant results. Also, the Lamas were only called by the rich as the required arrangements are very elaborate. While *dzizis* would come whenever summoned, the people would have to make an appointment with the Lama and a date would have to be fixed in advance for the puja. Today things have changed. People take such good care of the Lamas. They serve them with elaborate meals, give them at least a few hundred rupees and make them sit on fat cushion, while I, at times, have to sit on my own chappals.

Development has changed the equation between the *dzizi* and the common person. Today, in most of the Sherthukpen areas, people have access to outposts facilitating education, medicine and agriculture. Access to modern medicine and doctors certainly reduced the dependence on the *dzizi* as one of his chief roles was curative; and even today the *dzizi* is most frequently summoned to cure people of ill health. The spread of education and greater awareness resulted in a growing number of people to question their traditional belief system and seek tangible explanation. This also resulted in the surfacing of the negative impacts of consumption of large quantities of *phak* and other alcoholic drinks. *Phak* remains an essential ingredient in the rituals of the Sherthukpen priests and this growing awareness had an adverse effect on their further proliferation. Shift from slash and burn farming to settled agricultural practices resulted in greater predictability of harvests which affected the *dzizi's* existence as well.

The chief function of driving away evil spirits of the *dzizi* is also of lesser value in a world where the Sherthukpens no longer venture into the deep and mysterious forests as frequently as they used to. And, indeed, the forests are no longer as deep, dark and mysterious as they used to be. Many of the malicious forest spirits that were associated with certain areas of the forest are, therefore, no longer as fearful today and, thus, do not have to be mollified any longer. The clearing of forests has also contributed to the marginalisation of the *dzizi*.

As discussed above, Lamaism could also be a reason for the dwindling status of the Sherthukpen priests. The grand and organised nature of Lamaism attracted many to its folds. Also, in today's world, it is more respectable to be a follower of 'Buddhism' than some unknown animist faith whose priests cannot even be distinguished from the common man. The aura of Lamaism and a prominent figure like the Dalai Lama to represent it had an impact on the general psyche of the Sherthukpens. Gowloog notes,

> One of the most important developments that boosted Lamaism in Sikkim and relegated the traditional order to further oblivion was the settling of the Dalai Lama in India since 1959. This has been acknowledged by many observers to be responsible for the rejuvenation of the Lamaist order, in the whole of India.[22]

The Lamas, who were not very different from the local priests until then, began to receive more respect and attention.

Rumour has it that people are of the belief that the *dzizis* of today are not as powerful as the ones in the earlier days. During my time in the area, I heard a number of stories about competitions between powerful Lamas with *dzizis*. In the stories I heard, invariably, it was always the *dzizi* who won the exhibition of power and defeated the pompous Lama. However, interestingly, the element of nostalgia about the days when their *dzizi* was a more powerful figure could barely be concealed by the narrators. A palpable sympathy and affinity to their own faith was also discerned. A subtle propaganda launched by the Lamas against the indigenous religions can barely be ruled out from what was revealed by the head Lama of Rupa monastery. I was also told by many including Tshering Laam Dema and Karma of Rupa that the Rimpoche, or senior Lama, does not bless the *dzizi*. If a *dzizi* does go seeking blessings from a Rimpoche, he shows his thumb to the *dzizi*, and challenges him. This was also reported by some *dzizis* although such a claim could not be validated in my research.

Another point of reference could be the shunning of practices like animal sacrifice by the Lamas. Animal sacrifice was central to the ceremonies of the Lo. Although today they have been contained considerably, and in certain cases even stopped, but it must indeed have had an impact on the followers of the Lo. Not many years ago, under the influence of Lamaism and the principles laid down by the Dalai Lama, it was decided that the symbolic fish would not be sacrificed during the *Khiksaba*—the biggest Lo ceremony. Instead, the ceremony was conducted with the use of a flower. It is said that immediately after the ceremony, a storm of an intensity that had never been witnessed before, raged the environs of Rupa. It brought down the entire roof of the Rupa monastery. One of the metal sheets from the roof sliced the throat of a cow grazing in the grounds of the monastery. This is widely believed to be symbolic of the sacrifice that was not made during the *Khiksaba*. The year that followed was also marked by calamities, deaths and disasters. The people believe that the storm and the events that followed it were a symbol of the rage of their gods against the transgression of the *Khiksaba* rituals. The next year, *Khiksaba* was observed in its full splendour and the mandatory sacrifices were made to assuage the gods.

NOTES AND REFERENCES

1. *The Heathen in his Blindness* by S.N. Balagangadhara (1994), p. 138.
2. I have chosen to term the indigenous religion of the Sherthukpens as the Lo (even though the Sherthukpens themselves are not familiar with the term) because it was described as "the name of all the Sherthukpen gods and goddesses put together" by the senior-most Sherthukpen *dzizi* Tshering Norbu Dingla, of Rupa. I have not come across any other reference to the term. Haimendorf, however, describes the faith as the "Worship of Khik". This title is perhaps not the most accurate, and will be discussed in detail later in the chapter.
3. *Highlanders of Arunachal Pradesh: Anthropological Research in North-East India* by Christoph von Fürer-Haimendorf (1982), p. 174.

4. Written in the Devanagari script, *Pechha* may be described as Historical Treatises. The above-mentioned findings are based on the following *Pechhas*: Gapoe Kathang, Drukpa Choijung and Lhase Changma Namthar.
5. *Arunachal Panorama* by J.N. Chowdhury, p. 45.
6. *Highlanders of Arunachal Pradesh: Anthropological Research in North-East India* by Christoph von Fürer-Haimendorf (1982), p. 175.
7. Ibid., pp. 146-47.
8. *Lepchas of Sikkim* by Geoffrey Gorer (1987), p. 182.
9. *Highlanders of Arunachal Pradesh: Anthropological Research in North-East India* by Christoph von Fürer-Haimendorf (1982), pp. 148-49.
10. *The Buddhism of Tibet or Lamaism* by L.A. Waddell (1959), pp. 380-82, for the legendary history of Padmasambhava.
11. *Buddhism among the Monpas and Sherdukpens* by Niranjan Sarkar (1980), p. 1.
12. Ibid., p. 14.
13. Ibid., p. 14.
14. *Lepcha and their Heritage* by Tapan Chattopadhyay (1990).
15. The Dalai Lama belongs to the Gelukpa sect.
16. *Buddhism among the Monpas and Sherdukpens* by Niranjan Sarkar (1980), pp. 10-11.
17. Ibid., p. 12.
18. The *Khiksaba* is celebrated locally at Shergaon as well. It is the only other place, besides Rupa, that is allowed to observe *Khiksaba* celebrations. However, the festival at Shergaon is a small affair as compared to the celebrations at Rupa.
19. *Dongzur* is a two-storeyed stone shrine erected for the well-being of a group of people or *busti* people in the memory of a deceased person.

    Chorten is a solid stone structure that houses relics of a dead person and is believed to dispel evil spirits, misfortunes and diseases. Its construction is believed to add to the prosperity of the village.

    Maney is a crude and usually small stone wall built along the walking tracks and dirt roads. Tablets inscribed with *Om mani padme hum* are placed on *maneys* to protect the passers-by and remind them to recite the mantra. It is held that all creatures touched by the wind that passes over a *maney* take birth in a blessed place and are kept away from harm.
20. *The Sherdukpens* by R.R.P. Sharma (1961), p. 73.
21. See Social Organisation for detailed exploration.
22. *Lingthem Revisited* by Rip Roshina Gowloog (1995), p. 116.

6

Rites and Festivals

The Sherthukpens have a number of ceremonies and festivals which they celebrate ritually every year. The ceremonies are largely conducted by the Lamas or *dzizis* who, owing to their inherent or adopted powers, are believed to have an established communication with the spirit world. The ceremonies conducted by the Sherthukpens are mainly to foster good health, bountiful harvests, prosperity and well-being and to negate suffering and illness. The ceremonial procedures are either Lamaist in nature or belong to the indigenous rituals prescribed by the Lo. However, an overlapping of procedure and practice is discernable in both traditions. Today, as the dominion of Lamaism is greater in the region, it is the Lo ceremonies that are being fitted in a Lamaist mould. It is not unlikely that many of the festivals that are today presided over by the Lama are an adaptation of the indigenous Lo ceremonies and festivals that were traditionally conducted by the *dzizi*. While certain important ceremonies like the *Khiksaba* are highly elaborate, the more mundane rites and rituals remain rather simple and include proceedings such as the reading of holy books by the Lamas, making and painting of *tormas* or flour figures, burning of incense and the quintessential distribution of food and drink. It is also significant to note that a number of Sherthukpens who are poor or those who live in remote areas, do not summon the Lama on many of the occasions and events mentioned in this chapter. For many, a Lama may only be called upon at the event of death. However, an increasing number of Sherthukpens are being brought under the folds of Lamaism and an attempt is being made by the clergy to establish a more rigorous and active following among the Sherthukpens.

The elaborate festivities and ceremonies are largely conducted in Rupa. Sherthukpens living in the surrounding villages and hamlets come to celebrate the event at Rupa, as many of the ceremonies are not organised in the small villages and hamlets. Such a centralised mode of celebration does limit liberty at the village level but, in its place, these occasions offer to the people the opportunity to come together as a single community, and foster stronger ties and cultural homogeneity.

WANG

This two-day festival held in the summer months of June or July is celebrated by the Sherthukpens to pay homage to Lord Buddha. During the first day of the celebrations, elaborate images of Lord Buddha and other important Lamaist deities are prepared with wheat flour and coloured with *grima ku* or red dye traditionally obtained from the Monpas. The images of Lamaist gods are worshipped in an elaborate ceremony conducted by the Lamas held in the *gompa* on the first day. On the second day, the villagers are blessed by the Lamas and the rest of the day is spent in revelry and consumption of large quantities of food and drink prepared by the joint contribution of all the villagers. Food blessed by the gods, or *prasad,* is also distributed to all the households in the village.

BA JUNG KHLOBA

This simple ceremony is conducted by reading holy books and making *tormas* (figures of flour made by religious persons used for worship during festivals and ceremonies) before sending the cattle and other domesticated animals to the foothills before the winter migration. The *puja* is held to ensure the well-being of animals during migration. The gods are appeased to look after the animals and save them from catching a disease or epidemic.

The tradition of winter migration of the Sherthukpens has waned in the recent years and hardly anyone goes to Doimara any longer. Due to this factor, ceremonies and rites attached to the winter migration have suffered and do not have the same following as they enjoyed during the times when almost all the Sherthukpens would leave their highland dwellings and move to the warmer foothills for the winter.[1]

PHOTENYA

This is a simple harvest ceremony in which the *dzizi* ties strings of cereals in the temple and conducts a *puja* for the spirits of the forest and water bodies. The *dzizi* entreats the spirits to bless their land and fields and engender good harvests, prosperity and well-being. The spirits of the forest and water were appeased during *Photenya* because in the traditional times Sherthukpens practised rotational cultivation and cleared the forest land for fields. Irrigation was limited to either rainfall or the available water in the surrounding rivers. Hence, the bounty of both the forestland and water bodies was essential for a good harvest.

CHHOKAR

The Lamaist festival, also known as *Chhokar* or *Choikar* (*choi* – sacred books; *kor* – ritual circumambulation), is celebrated in the fourth month of the lunar calendar by the Sherthukpens. As prescribed by the name, the festival is marked by carrying the Lamaist sacred books in a ritual circumambulation. A service is held in the *gompa* during which the sacred texts are read by the Lamas for a period of six days. After this, on day seven, the Lamas and the villagers go around the village clockwise cutting across the adjoining fields and streams. The procession also covers the other holy spots in the village like the *dongzurs*. The sacred texts are mainly carried by the young unmarried women of the village who place the texts in a cloth and sling it on their backs or carry them on their heads. The procession halts from time to time and the people are served with *phak* and refreshments during the stops. The Aji Lamu dance is performed by some of the young Sherthukpen men. After the procession has gone around the village, some people go to other holy spots or *kros*.[2] In the evening people sit together and feast on food and drink. The young people go to their respective dormitories or *khubi nachao jingba* where they eat, drink and socialise. Some old people also visit the dormitories where they are made to drink large quantities of *phak* by the younger hosts.

The next day the Lama blesses the married women who have remained barren. These women walk around the *kro* thrice carrying a stone on their backs which is symbolic of conceiving a child. The men tease the women and mimic crying children. The women then return to their respective homes, carrying maize seeds on their backs. This practice is perceived as a good omen.

REK LAPSANG CHHONGBA

The agricultural deities are appeased during this ceremony conducted by a family or village in the event of unsatisfactory agricultural production. A ceremony that lasts for a few hours is conducted by a Lama, who reads the holy books in the fields and makes intricate *tormas* with red dye. A small number of *tormas* are flung in the field during the *puja* while some are eaten during the ceremony. The Lama appeases the agricultural deities and prays for the crops to be saved from the devastation caused by pests, rodents and wild animals.

JONKHLON

This ritual is held after the return of the Sherthukpens from Doimara. It is the time to plant new crops, a time for laborious agricultural work after the leisurely winter months spent at Doimara. The ritual conducted to appease the agricultural deities and rain gods is solemnised to engender healthy crops and ample rain.

TONU *WANG*

The ceremony of *Tonu Wang* is held before the *Khiksaba* when a few Sherthukpens are dispatched to Doimara to collect the requisite beetle nuts and *paan* leaves from the Kacharis that are used in the *Khiksaba* rituals. The ceremony is held to appease the forest spirits and ensure the well-being of the Sherthukpens who have to cut across the dense forested land for the journey.

LAAPSANG

Doimara became a permanent settlement in 1979. While people in the Sherthukpen belt go to Rupa to celebrate important events and festivals, the Sherthukpens of Doimara cannot easily do so owing to the distance and inaccessibility. The Sherthukpens at Doimara celebrate a festival that appeases the local deity Aiyo Sharmu. This is an old tradition, and even before the permanent settlement of the village, the Sherthukpens would come down from Rupa in the winter and perform the ceremony for the deity. This ceremony is also believed to engender well-being and keep people safe from harm. The *Gaonburah* of Doimara, Netan Dorje Thongon, said that after the performance of the *puja,* the hunts are always successful. He said that it was perhaps because in the *puja* people ask for the *apang* animals or those that have lost a limb and are, thus, of no use to the deity. *Laapsang* takes place after *Khiksaba* around the month of February. Rice, vegetables and other expenses for the ceremony are collected from the households in Doimara. No animal is sacrificed during the *puja;* however, a small piece of meat is used for conducting the necessary rituals. The GB[3] said a sheep used to be sacrificed for the ceremony but the practice was stopped about five years ago. He also said that when he was young, he was told by his elders that earlier a man used to be sacrificed in the name of the *devi.* Human sacrifice was gradually replaced by a sheep which, in turn, was exchanged for a piece of dry meat about five years ago. The ceremony is conducted by Lamas who are summoned from the monastery of Ningmadong, ahead of Dirang. These are Ningmapa monks who are often Monpas and at times Bhutanese. In 2004 the *puja* was held in late January and was conducted by three nuns from the *gompa.*

KHIKSABA

Khiksaba is the most important festival of the Sherthukpens and is celebrated only at the mother village of Rupa, in November or December. People from the entire Sherthukpen belt come to take part in the celebrations. The festival is also attended by some Kacharis who have long shared trade and barter relations with the Sherthukpens. The celebrations of the *Khiksaba* last for a period of seven days. On the first day of the festival, the *dzizi* performs prayers in the Kamcha or, the Lo temple at Rupa. For two days he coaches the younger *dzizis* in the esoteric Lo instruction. After this, the Panchayat gives a sheep to the *dzizi* who invites all the other *dzizis* with their families to his house where the sheep is cut by a servant and the meat prepared and eaten. The head of the sheep is taken to Newsuba—a spot in Rupa deemed holy by the practitioners of the Lo—and placed there after which two *dzizis* perform a *puja*. Two chickens are sacrificed and their blood is smeared over two *mamplo* or wooden sticks. These sticks are embedded in the ground facing each other after which the *dzizis* pass through the passage between them. No one is allowed to pluck out these sticks. The head of the sheep is left at the Newsuba. The *kachinpo* or servant comes to the spot with some *phak* or local beer for the *dzizis*.

Meanwhile, a woman from the Chao community prepares *phak* and food in the *gompa,* which is consumed by the *dzizis* after the ceremony at Newsuba. After eating the meal prepared at the *gompa,* the *dzizis* go to the gathering of the other *dzizis* and their families, and they jointly go for a picnic. After this, all the Sherthukpens gather under the holy trees at Rupa and the *dzizis* conduct a *puja* under three trees—Lablong, Chankon and Jamu.[4] The *dzizis* summon and mollify all the spirits and deities of the Lo during the ceremony and ask them to join them for the festivities of the *Khiksaba* and grant the Sherthukpens lasting prosperity and happiness. The forest deities, especially Phu Servi Mangbi, are appeased during the festival to ensure the safety of the Sherthukpens during the passage through the forested land on the journey to Doimara. After this ceremony the solemn affairs of the *Khiksaba* come to a close and the people eat, drink and rejoice throughout the day and night. The Khengpo dance,[5] among other traditional dances, is also performed on the occasion of the *Khiksaba*. The Sherthukpens traditionally left for Doimara shortly after the celebrations of the *Khiksaba*.

PHU-LAPSANG

Phu-lapsang is a ceremony performed to summon rain. This ceremony takes place when the rains are insufficient and the crops suffer owing to shortage of water. The ritual is performed by a Lama on hilltops. *Tormas* are prepared and a *puja* is conducted by chanting mantras and offerings of *phak,* grains and water to the rain deities. After the *puja,* the villagers sit and eat and drink together.

BIRTH RITES

There are no strict birth rites observed by the Sherthukpens. According to *dzizi* Tshering Norbu Dingla, traditionally there were no rites or rituals observed on the occasion of a child's birth because newborn children were considered unclean and hence the *dzizis* did not perform any birth rites. On the day of the birth of a child in the Sherthukpen community, women of the same clan as well as other women from the village visit the mother and child with an offering of *phak* that they give to the mother. On the third day, the women visit the newborn again and with the tail of a fish, put a few drops of *phak* into the baby's mouth and bless the baby with ceremonial scarves. A male child is also given a gift of bow and arrow by the visiting women. No male is allowed to be a part of this gathering. The father is tabooed from touching the child for the first seven days. The mother, on the other hand, is forbidden from touching any of the dishes or articles in the kitchen. She is also not allowed to bathe for the first two days after giving birth. Delivery of a child takes place in a confined corner of the house and a Thong mother is traditionally helped by an elderly Chao woman attached to her clan, as well as other women of the family. A Chao woman is assisted in her delivery only by other women of her clan and family. These traditional rules, however, are no longer strictly adhered to today and many Thong women deliver babies without the attendance of a Chao woman.

With the adoption of Lamaism, people have started to observe the Lamaist birth rites. On the third day after the birth of a child, the father of the newborn goes to a Lama with a gift of *phak* to chart out the newborn's horoscope and give it a name. On the fifth day, the Lama performs a ceremony known as *nenui satpa*. The child is brought out in the open and the Lama conducts a *puja* sitting in the balcony of the house. A small feast is organised for the clan members and the women who had assisted the mother during childbirth are sent off with gifts. When the child is one year old, the Lama is again summoned for the hair-cutting ceremony, which is performed only by the maternal grandfather of the child. In his absence, the maternal uncle too may cut the child's hair. The process is simple. The maternal grandfather or uncle of the child takes a pair of scissors and cuts the child's hair which is preserved in the house by the parents. The uncle or grandfather is served with a lavish meal and drinks and he is sent off the same day. The Lama who presides over the ceremony does not have a major role to play at the event; however, his presence is believed to add a measure of sanctity to the occasion.

DEATH RITES

Sherthukpens are either buried or cremated. More often, the rich are cremated while the poor Sherthukpens bury their dead. A child, irrespective of the economic status of his parents, is always buried. When a Sherthukpen dies, the grown-up men and women of the village gather in the house of the deceased to console the remaining family members and express their sorrow. All the male clan members are required to take off their headgear while the women remove their jewellery and upbraid their hair. The family members immediately dispatch a messenger to deliver the news to his in-laws' family. It is important that the father-in-law, mother-in-law, maternal uncle, clan members and some Chaos attached to the clan of the deceased are in attendance while the last rites are being performed. A Lama is also sent for soon after the death has taken place; he, according to the time, place, cause and nature of the death, consults the holy books and prescribes the place and direction of disposing off the dead body. A Thong is prohibited from touching a corpse; therefore, a Thong dead body is washed and wrapped by the Chaos attached to the clan of the Thong.

In case of a burial, the Chaos attached to the Thong family wash the body, cream the face with some yak butter and wrap a piece of clean cloth around it. Chaos also fetch the wood and construct the bier to carry the dead body.[6] They place the corpse on the bier while a Chao woman prepares a meal and *phak* for herself and the dead person, which is carried along with the body to the site of cremation. The Chao woman herself serves in the dishes used by the dead person just before dying. She eats from these dishes, which are later given to her by the Thong family. The Lama conducts a *puja* before the body is carried out of the main door and fastened to the bier. The bier is carried to the place of cremation by four Chao men who walk along with the funeral procession with the Lama, maternal uncle, the widow with her children, clan members and the father-in-law. The Lama conducts a ceremony after placing the corpse on the pyre. He offers food to the diseased after which the widow and her children walk around the pyre three times. The widow and then her children light the pyre after which everyone except the Lama and some Chaos return to the village. The Chaos collect the ash after the body has burnt and immerse it in a river. They return to the house where the death has taken place and are offered food and money in return for their assistance. The family observes a number of precautions and taboos like not eating deep-fried food for the first seven days. The ceremonial mourning period lasts for 21 days, during which the concerned household refrains from performing agricultural work and other economic activities. The clan members also observe this taboo for three days after the death has taken place.

On the seventh day after the demise of a person, the Lama performs another ceremony called the *Kro* in the village monastery. The widow and her children light butter lamps in the monastery and the Lama reads from the holy books. A prayer flag is erected in the village *gompa* after which an elaborate feast is prepared for all the villagers by the family of the deceased. The father-in-law and the maternal uncle are sent off on this day after the feast. The Chao women who have been of assistance are rewarded as well. Flags are also installed on day 14 and 21 under the instructions of the presiding Lama. Then, depending upon the economic status of the family, prayer ceremonies are arranged in different religious shrines and the Lamas are offered food, drink and gifts. Traditionally, the well-off would give the Lamas offerings of a cow or horse and silver cups among other gifts. The *Kro* ceremony is considered highly significant and all Sherthukpens, irrespective of their class or economic status, have to perform it, although the ceremony may be less elaborate when conducted by the poor.

NOTES AND REFERENCES

1. The winter migration has been described in detail by R.R.P. Sharma in *The Sherdukpens* (1961) as well as in the *Census of India Report* (1971).
2. *Kro* is a cave. Caves have been significant in the Sherthukpen religion since very early times. The Sherthukpens hold certain caves in their area as holy. Earlier, some caves were also used to dispose off the dead.
3. *Gaonburah.*
4. There was a fourth holy tree in Rupa called Kho, which perished some years ago.
5. See architecture for details.
6. The body of a dead child is not placed on the bier. A Chao male carries it to the burial ground in his arms or on his back.

7

Indigenous Knowledge

Despite the growing recognition of the value of Indigenous Knowledge (IK) for sustainable development, it has not yet been widely incorporated into the research and development processes. In the last two decades, research and development experts have promoted indigenous knowledge as a key to sustainable development. Dr. Gupta, of IIM Ahmedabad, who has been working on IK for the past 15 years, is of the opinion that indigenous communities, tribes and rural farmers might be economically poor but are rich in IK. This knowledge, if used effectively, could result in raising the economic standard of these communities.[1] Unfortunately, many corporate houses and conglomerates like Dabur think nothing of stealing indigenous wealth, marketing it and giving not a penny back to the rightful holders of that knowledge. A wealth of information on indigenous knowledge pertaining to soils, plants and animals has been compiled in the last two decades. Even so, integration of IK into the research process and its application within the development context remains highly scarce.

A rationale for this lack is the dominance of scientific knowledge, making it cryptic for those trained in Western science and development experts to deal with a different knowledge system. An elementary disparity between indigenous and scientific knowledge is that while science is in the quest of information of universal import, which is not context-related, IK is conversely a social product which is intrinsically linked or even restricted to a cultural and environmental context. This, in turn, implies that IK is dynamic and evolving as the collective experience of definite social groups in relation with their immediate environment. Another significant difference between IK and modern knowledge systems is that while in the former, the creators and users are the same indigenous people, the latter is, by and large, the result of industrialisation processes where knowledge is commonly created for wider use and profit. Consequently, we see that in the case of IK, the sustainable use of raw materials or biodiversity on which knowledge is applied to create useful products and services is in-built. While, in the case of modern knowledge, the creators as well as the users are detached from the sustainability of resources. This elucidates the need and urgency to incorporate IK into research processes.

LANGUAGE

The Sherthukpens speak the Sherthukpen dialect. It is a preliterate language that is said to belong to the Tibeto-Burman school of languages. The Sherthukpen dialect has not been studied in detail by philologists so far. A study of this nature has to be conducted for greater revelations. However, broadly, the Sherthukpens of Rupa and those of Shergaon speak dialects that have slight variations. People are of the opinion that the Sherthukpen spoken in Shergaon is a little more polite and sweet-sounding as compared to that of Rupa—father's younger brother is *ache* in Rupa and *aku* in Shergaon. A local legend has it that the third son of Japtang Bura settled down in Shergaon and married a Monpa girl of Dirang district. Being married to the third son of Bura added to her prestige in society and the admixture spoken by her—Sherthukpen with her mother tongue—resulted in considerable impact on the language spoken at Shergaon. The Shergaon Sherthukpen is said to have a marked influence of the Monpa dialect and this influence is believed to go back to this marriage alliance.

The Sherthukpen and Monpa dialects are said to have certain similarities in their lilt and lexicon. The dialect spoken by the people of Michhopo, But, Rahung, Khudum and Khoina has "great similarities to that of Sherthukpens on casual observation," says Sharma.[2] He adds,

> People being predominantly Buddhists, the use of Tibetan in Tibetan script on prayer flags, Manes, Kakalings and Gompas is fairly common in Sherthukpen area, but it is extremely doubtful if anybody, except the initiated brotherhood, can read and understand it.[3]

Tibetan is indeed known to very few lay persons; and as discussed earlier,[4] the number of Sherthukpens adopting Lamahood is restricted to a few. After the adoption of Lamaism, the use of Tibetan in the religious and ceremonial rites of the Sherthukpens has seen a considerable increase. Some Sherthukpens are of the opinion that this is a setback to their community as they cannot wholeheartedly participate in the ceremonies, which are now entirely rendered in a foreign tongue. Some people were also of the opinion that it distanced the common man from the Lama and was an impediment in their spiritual growth. People felt that this catered to the esoteric hocus-pocus image of the Lamas, some of whom benefited directly from continuation of Tibetan as a cryptic language. This is so because every household that has a Buddhist alter with sacred books in their home has to ritually summon Lamas to read the books as they themselves cannot read them. Norm has it that the Lamas have to be inundated with luscious foods and drinks and thus the ritual requires high expenditure. The owners of a well-known private school in Rupa seem to be aware of this lacuna. So much so that they have introduced Tibetan as a separate subject in the curriculum of their school. What's more, the lady in charge and her sister have started private lessons and are learning to read and write Tibetan as well. She was of the opinion that, "Knowledge of the language will enhance our understanding of the religion and once we can read the script, our dependence upon the Lamas will decrease as well."

Sherthukpens are natural linguists. Owing to their long-standing relationship with the Kacharis and their proximity to Assam, many Sherthukpens are conversant in Assamese. However, the people of NEFA, much like others living in the hill districts of erstwhile Assam, did not take kindly to being force-fed in Assamese. Das observes,

> The process of disintegration of Assam (caused due to the identity assertion of different tribal minorities of the hill districts in response to the attempt of forced Assamisation through the imposition of Assamese language upon them) started with the creation of Nagaland as a separate state.[5]

He adds,

> In the field of language and religion, preceding two decades witnessed a rapid integration. Following the popular demand of the local people English was adopted as the medium of instruction along with Hindi. In fact, Assamese was replaced by Hindi even in the sphere of inter-tribal communities. Extension of television transmission facilities even in far-flung border areas and fast growing video hall business have popularised Hindi all over the territory. Hindi movies are also displayed in the border villages by the defence officials. Apart from Hindi, Sanskrit is also being introduced in academic curriculum recently. Similarly, following the rapid growth of activities of Hindu missions, many Hindu gods and goddesses have been adopted by the local tribal population...[6]

Today, many Sherthukpens especially in the semi-urban settlements also speak Hindi and, to a lesser extent, English. This is a direct consequence of the introduction of Hindi and English in the educational system, and the induction of mainstream monoculture via popular media.

The army settlement nearby Rupa runs a cinema hall in the town which is open to civilians. Residents of Rupa take pride in mentioning that their town boasts of a cinema hall while even the district headquarters of Bomdila does not have one. Sherthukpens, much like many other people of Arunachal Pradesh, relish Bollywood cinema and more so Hindi film songs. In my opinion, Bollywood has indeed played an important role in giving a common point of reference to Indians from different states. Bollywood reigns and rejoices people even in some of the most remote pockets of our diverse country. While in Rupa, I would often sit by the main street in the morning hours and watch streams of schoolchildren in uniform pass by swinging their hands joyously and singing popular Bollywood tunes. I must confess that in spite of being a part of the 'Indian mainstream', whatever that might be, my knowledge of film songs was amateurish compared to that of the young Sherthukpens. Television is commonplace in the semi-urban settlements of Rupa and Shergaon as well, and has added to the further popularisation of not only Hindi but mainstream Hindu morality as well. However, according to the Minister of State D.K. Thongdok, the influx of the mainstream media has only a temporary impact on the Sherthukpens. "It is only a passing phase. Our identity is under no threat from the media", he asserts. In my observation, however, this statement seems a little too ambitious. Many young Sherthukpens and Monpas, and most other Arunachalese, seem to increasingly emulate the mainstream and are a little insecure about their indigenous culture. Much like how the mainstream tends to copy the West and is insecure about their own identity.

Here, I would like to recount an experience during my fieldwork. On the occasion of the festival *Chotta Losar,* I was escorted to a Monpa village a few hours from Bomdila by a girl who had studied in the high school of that village. However, as the school was not up to the level of senior secondary, she had to move to Bomdila for further education. At the time of the event, the girl had been out of the village for about two years and was in class 12. She took me to her village, escorted me to the quaint monastery and pointed out the extraordinary vistas visible from her highland village. Later, we visited the homes of many of her relatives to participate in the festive occasion and eventually went to her grandmother's house for dinner. However, by the time we reached the house it was late and the family had already eaten. On seeing us, the ladies, preparing for their nightly slumber, immediately scurried off to prepare our meal. In a matter of about half an hour, we were served with a piping hot meal of yak, radish, rice and chilli chutney. As the evening progressed, however, I noticed the reluctance of my escort in communicating with her family members. Later, after bidding our farewell, we left for Bomdila in the quiet of the night; sitting in the taxi I tried to question my companion on her unlikely behaviour. Her answer to my questions was that after spending two years in Bomdila, she was no longer comfortable speaking in her mother tongue and even claimed to have forgotten most of it.

This behaviour is perhaps commonplace among people across the country, who are increasingly trying to adopt an urban lifestyle and connect to the mainstream, thereby shrugging off whatever rural affiliations they might have. However, the repercussions of such denial on a small tribal community could be graver in terms of loss of tradition as compared to that of, say, the populous states of India's vast *chapaati* belt of Bihar and UP. Also, these developments being new in the highlands, it is too soon to calmly proclaim, "It is only a passing phase." Such digressions should be taken more seriously and efforts to revive and popularise the Sherthukpen language, especially among the young, should be made. Singular emphasis should be laid upon the language as it is among the most enduring and binding factors of a small community; once the language is lost, there remain few other points of commonality that bind a community as a solitary unit. This could be done profitably with the help of bodies like the Sherthukpen Youth Association and the introduction of interactive activities of indigenous interest in schools and colleges that revive pride in indigenous practices. But this is not in accordance with the integration policy adopted by the centre. This implies that greater introspection on these issues is needed at the level of the district, state as well as the centre.

FOLKLORE

The Sherthukpens have a rich repository of folklore. Their folk traditions reveal rare poetic imagination and aesthetics of a mild-mannered people. The Sherthukpen world was created by two celestial brothers who held sway over the skies, though none was the almighty. They created the earth by the gentle act of throwing a lotus from the sky upon the primeval ocean. Beauty is eulogised in their lore and there is a marked fascination for colour; rainbows abound and different spirits are defined less by their powers and more by their colour. The many coloured water spirits loiter around the skies, forming rainbows, in pursuit of their mates. There are kings, queens, demons and ogres, and descriptions of different lands, a land of dogs and another where only lascivious women dwell; there are also references to different evolutionary patterns and a lore recounts a tale of a time when men and women were so tiny that they could be carried off and devoured by birds. Harmony prevails even in unlikely circumstances and at times the righteous kings and queens can be found dancing together in joyful abandon along with the demons. The element of enquiry about the origin of the earth, fire, water, earthquakes exists. The logic behind the design of things is simple, and only modest emphasis is laid upon the patterns of sin and morality. Yet, the good is habitually seen to prevail.

Story-telling was a favourite pastime of the Sherthukpens inhabiting the unrelenting highlands, and stories abound on topics significant to the lives of these people. There are tales about their priests or *dzizis*, Lamas and sorcerers, kings and queens, hunters and fish, yaks, deer, elephants, snakes, birds and mosquitoes and dim-dam flies, many of which are recounted in their colourful dance and music traditions. There is an evident influence of Lamaism in Sherthukpen lore.

> The Buddhist or near-Buddhist tribes have a developed civilisation which has been considerably influenced by Tibet and Burma. In western Kameng live the Monpas and Sherdukpens, gentle, courteous people who cultivate on terraces, maintain large number of cattle, sheep and horses and are to a great extent under the influence of the Lamasery of Tawang. Both tribes combine in their religion and mythology traditional tribal ideas with the Buddhist theology.[7]

Elwin observes

> NEFA traditions about the Creation of the world are of five main types, all of which can be paralleled in both the classical and the tribal literature of India... Very common is the idea that the world arose from a primeval ocean or was formed upon its surface.[8]

Elwin does not rule out the possibility of some external influence on the folklore of the people of NEFA. He notes,

> It is remarkable that people who have never seen the sea nor even, so far as we can tell, large sheets of water of any kind, should have devised the idea of a primeval ocean from which all things have emerged. This tradition, of course, is as old as the Upanishads... from Bori, Gallong, Hill Miri, Nocte, Sherthukpen, Minyong and Taraon Mishmi stories describe how at first everything was water... Among the Sherthukpens, it is believed that two heavenly brothers threw a lotus down onto the surface of the ocean, whereupon it was covered with flowers, over which the four winds blew clouds of dust until the earth was formed.[9]

He later adds that neither of the two brothers is the Supreme Being. "It is interesting to note that the creation of the world is not usually attributed to a Supreme Being, but to lesser gods who often act in pairs."[10] This could be an indication of a mindset that is not in support of being governed by a central power. In practice, however, the Sherthukpens are governed by TVC which is rather centralised.

Here it might be mentioned that, in my observation, the folklore tradition of the Sherthukpens seems to belong to two distinct segments and, arguably, time periods. The Sherthukpen tales that are dedicated to the aforementioned aspects dealing with the knowledge and curiosity of creation of the earth, spirits, demons, men and women, fire, water, etc. seem to be more primordial in nature than the set of legends belonging to the life and times of their ancestor Japtang Bura. These, going by their comparative sophistication and shift in focus, might have been a later addition to the existing folklore of the Sherthukpens. Another rationale to elucidate this divide could be that while many Sherthukpens are familiar with some of the lore attached to Japtang Bura, hardly anyone, young or old, can recollect legends of, what in my opinion could be classified as the former set. However, I have found no references to support this division and argument.

Unfortunately, even the *dzizis* today can barely recollect their lore in any detail. Most people do not seem to remember their folklore and had it not been for the singular attempt of Elwin who documented a range of Sherthukpen tales in his *Myths of NEFA*, the task of compiling the Sherthukpen lore would have been an impossible one. Much of the above information has been furnished with reference to Elwin's book as I could only obtain patchy details of the Sherthukpen lore during my fieldwork. Most of the old people seem to have forgotten these ancient tales as well—a treasure-trove of the vivid imagination of their forefathers. Furthermore, these stories belong to oral tradition and thus it is difficult to ascertain the more authentic version. Nevertheless, the one lore that almost every Sherthukpen, young or old, can recount is that of their legendary ancestor Japtang Bura, related earlier in the report.[11] The other traditional tales seem to have been long forgotten. This could be due to the shift of interest from storytelling to other means of entertainment—the most popular being television, gambling, card games and popular media. It appears that the young generation of Sherthukpens seems to have isolated themselves from the age-old tradition of storytelling altogether.

For the purpose of brevity, the tales documented by Elwin are not being reproduced in this report, as, indeed it would be of greater merit to refer to the original source. The following comprise tales that do not find mention in the *Myths of NEFA*. However, with no comparable data for reference, it is difficult to authenticate the tales. Being passed down from generations orally, these can, at best, be taken as an interpretation of an informed individual which have been validated by a number of other people.

The Snake of Chingy and the Legend of Khing-Thong

Once, Japtang Bura was journeying his kingdom and reached a hamlet called Chingy.[12] To his astonishment, Bura found the dwelling totally deserted of any sign of life. The streets were empty, and no cries of children emanated from any of the homes that lined the streets. Curious, Bura swung off his horse and started to pace the village. Finally, he turned into the last street of the village and to his relief saw rings of smoke wafting from a chimney of a small house in the corner. Bura walked to the front door of the house which was left ajar, and he peeped inside to see an old woman and her daughter crying bitterly over a plateful of food with their foreheads touching each other's. As the shadow of Japtang fell upon the two women, they turned to face him and were taken aback to see the big stately man standing at their front door. He succeeded in calming them down and asked them to divulge the cause of their sorrow.

Slowly, between fits of sobs, the mother and daughter told Bura that their entire village had been tormented by a leviathan snake known as Miderlabde. He had devoured scores of people in the village till the villagers decided to let him eat one person from the village everyday so that the others may live in relative peace. This process had been going on for some time; and only the two women were left alive in the entire village as the snake had engulfed all the other inhabitants of the village one by one. The mother and daughter were both insisting on being the first to go to the snake and were thus crying over their last meal together. Japtang heard the sad saga of the village and went into deep thought. He then told the two that he and his soldiers were hungry and enquired if they could get some food. Bura and his men were fed by the women, after which he declared that the mother and daughter had nothing to fear and that he would protect them. Bura then lay in wait for the menacing snake's arrival. As the evening approached, the snake eventually came to the front door of the house, and as soon as he pushed open the door and opened his mouth to swallow one of the women, Bura shot numerous poisoned arrows into the mouth of the snake. The wounded snake recoiled and slithered away to the region of the two great lakes from where Je Dinkho[13] originates. Bura and his men followed the snake and upon reaching the land of the two lakes Bura saw, to his great surprise, a Lama meditating on a rock by the lakes. By then, the snake had entered one of the lakes which was shaking violently with the impact of the reptile. Bura walked up to the meditating Lama who told him that he was called Tanpe Dema and had been praying for the past many years to control the snake that had caused such widespread devastation, but had not succeeded in his endeavour so far. He thanked Bura and his cavalry of men for exterminating the evil snake. However, the expedition had made Bura and his men hungry and thirsty, and they asked the Lama if they could get some food from him. The Lama gave them a portion of his *bhukpi*. It was a meagre quantity for Bura and his men; however, they ate what they were offered without complaint and upon eating the scanty amount of *bhukpi* they realised that they were well satisfied and felt neither hunger nor thirst. The *bhukpi* worked like a *jinlaap* or, food that provides the ultimate satisfaction. Bura then realised that this could be no ordinary Lama and that he was irrefutably in august company. Bura sought his blessings and the Lama and Bura parted cordially. Legend has it that Guru Rimpoche Tulku Gonpashe of the Old Gompa, or monastery, in Bomdila is the reincarnation of this Lama.

Bura returned to the house in the village and to his surprise saw that the Lama was already sitting there talking to the two women. He informed the mother and daughter that the snake had been eliminated and they could now live their lives in peace. It was late and Bura and his men spent the night in the house with the intention of marching ahead the next day. He noticed the radiant smile on the girl's face after she heard the good news and Bura was so charmed that he seduced her after everyone else had gone to bed. The next morning, Bura and his men left for their onward journey. After this event, in time, the girl gave birth to Bura's son. However, Bura had forgotten about the girl and his son grew up in the village without the knowledge of his father's existence. One day he implored his mother to divulge the identity of his father. The mother eventually told her son to set out on a journey and follow the river Dumkho. She then commanded him to also trail the next river that would join Dumkho. Finally, she described the physical characteristics of his father and asked him to go and look for his father if he so desired. He set off on the journey and in due course reached Rupa and accomplished his mission of finding his father Japtang Bura. He approached him and succeeded in convincing Bura that he was his son. By this time, Japtang had had many sons, and on realising that the boy before him was also his son, he felt a little cornered. However, he acknowledged his son, and asked him not to live with him in Rupa but instead settle in the village Kling. The son did as he was told and started to rule the Kling village. The legend goes that the son, not used to power and its pitfalls, in time, became proud and tyrannical and started to oppress his people. He married a girl from Rupa of the Migeji[14] clan and became so engulfed in his own importance that he declared himself as the Kling-Thong or the King of Kling, and forbade anyone from outside to enter into his territory. The stories of his tyranny reached Japtang's ears and he decided to send an army to subdue him. He was killed in the encounter and his pregnant wife was saved by her Migeji clan brothers who brought her back to Rupa. She later gave birth to a son who went on to serve the Thongs and thus redeemed the dishonour brought to his mother's clan by his father's actions.

I was unable to ascertain the clan of the mother of the ruler of Kling, but in all likelihood it seems that the girl Japtang Bura had seduced must belong to the Chao clan, as there seems to be an undertone of Thong supremacy in the legend and the reinforement of traditional clan hierarchy.

MEDICINE

The people in preliterate societies with beliefs in shamanist-animist faiths mainly employ two indigenous methods when inflicted with ill-health: They either summon the medicine man who cures the ill by the use of local herbs, or they seek help from their village priests to perform curative ceremonies via exorcism and propitiation of spirits. The practice of exorcism as a cure is owing to the psychological support provided to the patient from the larger commune—the ill are not held responsible for their state which is deemed the intervention of supernatural elements. Traditionally, the Sherthukpens too either summoned the *dzizi* for curative techniques or sought help from the local medicine practitioners. The Sherthukpens had a fairly wide knowledge of the curative qualities of various plants and animals found in their immediate vicinity; however, based on the findings of my fieldwork, it may be said that this indigenous wealth never evolved into a specialised branch of knowledge or practice. Nevertheless, certain individuals, owing to their interest in the healing qualities of plants and animals, became better known than others in being able to cure people of illness, or specific illnesses.

Little of what once could have been a vast Sherthukpen reservoir of medicinal knowledge remains today. This is true over and above the fact that the use of modern medication in the region is mainly a post-independence phenomenon. Curiously, in a matter of a few decades, their traditional medicinal knowledge has eroded considerably. This is largely due to the unspecialised nature of the practice as well as the combined consequence of deteriorating forests, imposition of strict forest rules and regulations, shift from trade and barter practices to the monetary economy and slash and burn farming to settled cultivation, changes in lifestyle and the far-reaching influences of modernity. The knowledge has deteriorated faster also because the practice was widely scattered and often limited to specific ailments; different practitioners excelled in curing only specific ailments. What was incurable was often deemed the result of supernatural malevolent action and thus needed intervention from the *dzizi* who would perform ceremonies and rites to pacify the spirit.

Being mainly from an oral tradition, the medicinal knowledge of the Sherthukpens was not recorded in any permanent manner and thus the wealth of medicinal know-how that has been lost is irrecoverable. Medicinal techniques were passed down from one enthusiast to another, mainly from an older and experienced practitioner to a budding incumbent who would, in turn, divulge his knowledge to others before the end of his days. There was no organised form of returns to be paid to the medicine men for their services. However, people reciprocated by giving to the medicine man whatever they could. The returns were commonly agricultural produce, firewood, etc. It might be said that no grave reciprocal demands were inherent to this practice. This was because the Sherthukpens lived as a community and supported each other in times of need. Medical knowledge was not just an asset of the practising individual but also of the community at large. Interestingly, this aspect of the medicinal tradition has seen little variation even today. However, people make payments both in cash or kind.

In the present times, the Sherthukpens are increasingly seeking medical help from modern hospitals and health centres. But still many of the people continue to prescribe to their indigenous beliefs in matters related to health and patronise both the *dzizi* and local medicine man. This is not only true for the remote inaccessible Sherthukpen pockets where, indeed, it is not extremely convenient to seek the help of modern doctors; but this observation is as true for the semi-urban settlements of Rupa and Shergaon, both of which have modern health outposts. Ironically, while the practice of the medicine man has witnessed sizable decline and has been replaced by modern doctors and medicine, the belief in the *dzizi* in matters pertaining to ill-health is widespread even among the educated Sherthukpens of today. Many educated Sherthukpens, both young and old, were of the belief that they had witnessed many cases in which the *dzizi* had miraculously cured a patient of suffering. Is this perhaps an indication of the continuing superstitious bent of mind of the Sherthukpens? Or, arguably, are the esteemed esoteric powers of the local priests unexplored in the realms of mainstream knowledge?

Here, we will mainly contend with the employment of curative techniques with the use of herbs and other substances used by the local Sherthukpen medicine man. Much of the information in this section is a result of an interview with

Namgay Sinchaji, of Rupa, who is widely regarded to offer an alternative to allopathic medication. He is especially known for his expertise in ailments related to bones. Namgay Sinchaji is a stately old man of 64. He lives in a traditional one-room Sherthukpen house in a joint family setup. During my time in Rupa, he was himself suffering from an illness but in spite of his obvious discomfort, he continued to maintain a joyous countenance and even attempted to treat people who came to him, as well as entertained my repeated queries with immense patience. He informed me that it was the old people who would commonly go to the forest to collect medicinal plants.

> When I was young, the older people used to know a lot about the medicinal plants and animals in our forests. These people were not specialised practitioners but did it more out of interest and need. There was no medicine man as such except for the dzizi. Those people have all died now. The children these days seldom venture into the forest and the knowledge our ancestors had has died and people are content eating hospital tablets.

Common Cures

Fracture

Herb used – *Hanganiya*

Process – The ruptured or broken bone is stretched and aligned in place. The affected part is then drummed with a red hot iron rod called *mikcha*. The root of the creeper known as *hanganiya* that climbs around tall trees has to be obtained from the forest. Sinchaji said that getting these tubers from the forest was a backbreaking chore as these creepers are extremely difficult to dislodge. Once the tubers have been collected from the forest, they are cut, heated and mashed, and the potion spread around the fractured part like an ointment. This potion automatically becomes hard on cooling and serves the purpose of a cast. No additional plaster or bandage is required for this treatment. It is widely held that this indigenous cure to fractures is more effective than the one in hospitals.

Fever

Herb used – *Machank*

Process – M*achank* plants are commonly of two varieties and sizes. Both varieties can be used to cure fever. The leaves of the plant have to be boiled. After letting the leaves boil for a few minutes, the water is seived and consumed for relief from fever.

Stomach Ache

Herb used – *Bay*

Process – *Bay* is a ginger-like tuber, slightly smaller in size. This tuber is eaten raw for relief from stomach ache. Consuming the tuber or even carrying it is believed to keep evil spirits away.

Body Ache/ Headache

Animal used – Bear, Yak

Process – The meat of a bear is highly valued among the Sherthukpens not only for its flavour and taste but also because of the many healing qualities present in the meat. Bear oil or fat is said to cure even the most obstinate body pains. Sinchaji said that the oil or fat of a yak can also be used for the same purpose. However, only the fat/oil of yaks without horns has medicinal qualities and not that of the yaks with horns. Bear oil/fat, however, is said to be superior to yak oil or fat.

Joint pains

Animal Used – Wild boar, bear

Process – Oil extracted from a wild boar is said to relieve people of joint pains. However, bear oil is believed to have greater curative powers.

Hair loss

Animal used – Bear

Process – Massaging the head with bear oil is said to stop hair loss and help engender hair growth.

Cracked heels, body sores

Herb used – Pine

Process – The gum of the pine tree is collected and heated on slow fire. The heated gum is applied over affected parts for relief. During times when the Sherthukpens did not commonly wear shoes, the foot cracks and body sores mainly caused by the severe cold were often healed with the use of pine gum.

Namgay Sinchaji added that his signature cure of treating fractures and other bone-related problems was an indigenous practice which was passed down to him by two Sherthukpens—an old man from Chillipam, and a *Gaonburah* of Rupa. Sinchaji had learnt these techniques from these people when he was about 20 years old and was told by his teachers that even they had learned the cure from other Sherthukpens. Sinchaji was certain that the treatment was originally Sherthukpen as he was familiar with the treatment procedure of the Monpas and other neighbouring tribes. He also reaffirmed that their treatment could not have come from Bhutan because he was well-versed with the Bhutanese indigenous cures. According to Sinchaji, Bhutanese Lamas commonly cure bone problems with oil massages, reciting of mantras and hot iron treatment. In light of the above evidences, it may be said that the treatment is indigenous to Sherthukpens. However, it is very difficult to ascertain whether all the above-mentioned cures are native to the Sherthukpens. The Sherthukpens share a marked cultural affinity with the Monpas and hence influences on medicinal practices cannot be ruled out, especially during times when the people had no ready access to doctors or hospitals and indigenous medication was among the chief alternatives. Consequently, influences from the Bhutanese, Tibetan, Akas, Khowas and Kacharis, among others, in the medicinal practice of the Sherthukpens are a likelihood.

OIL EXTRACTION

The Sherthukpens have an age-old system of oil extraction. Traditionally, the Sherthukpens did not use oil in their daily diet; the method employed for the purpose was laborious and hence oil extraction took place only on occasions of special significance and celebration. Interestingly, the Sherthukpens devised not one but a range of methods to extract oil. It is difficult to say whether the various methods and ingredients engaged by the people to extract oil have all survived the times, as today, with the cropping up of markets in the mountainous Sherthukpen terrain, this indigenous method is seldom put to task. Gradually, with the change from trade and barter practices to a monetary economy, better communication, roads and transportation and the spread of semi-urban settlements in the area, there was little need to extract oil as the same began to be available in the nearby market places. However, there is evidence to show that the knowledge of oil extraction in the Sherthukpen belt was widespread and it was practised on occasions throughout the Sherthukpen area till some decades ago. I was also told that on rare occasions Sherthukpens, especially those living in the remote pockets, obtain oil by employing indigenous methods even today. However, during my time in the area I could not witness any such practice. I also did not come across any household that was using home-made oil for domestic consumption.

According to my information, the different methods of oil extraction were primarily based on the same technique and did not differ dramatically from each other. However, Sherthukpens obtained oil from five types of plants—*jomotho, dhamphik, sengmaar, heengbachche* and *nyagmaar*—with the most common being a local variety of mustard or *jomotho*. The Sherthukpens extracted oil from the local mustard grown in the area. Oil was extracted by first drying mustard flowers in the sun. The dried seeds were then beaten on a bamboo mat or any large container and separated from the rest of the flower. The collected seeds were roasted over slow fire. These seeds were then placed in a round cane vessel called *cher*. The seeds were pressed and tightly packed with some heavy stones and a curved pine stick was strategically placed in the *cher*. After this process, the *cher* was opened from the top and the oil was made to flow down slowly from the curved pine stick and was collected in a vessel. This oil was filtered with the help of a fine cloth before use.

Jomotho – Oil is extracted from this local mustard plant variety. Mustard oil is the cooking medium commonly used by the Sherthukpens. However, these days it is purchased from the market.

Dhamphik – These are mustard-like brownish plants that are cultivated for the extraction of oil. The seeds in the flowering plants are used to obtain edible oil. Additionally, *dhamphik* seeds can also be consumed raw in place of butter.

Sengmaar – The pea-like fruits growing on tall *sengmaar* trees in the forests abounding in the Sherthukpen belt were used to extract oil. However, owing to the degradation of forests, these trees are not as commonly found in the woods any longer.

Heengbachche – The Sherthukpens extracted oil from a pine-like tree known as *heengbachche* which engenders a gum used for oil extraction. The oil extracted from this gum is not liquid but in semi-solid form and resembles chunks of charcoal. These chunks turn into fluid when heated. According to the people, the oil of *heengbachche* was greatly savoured for its rich flavour and smell. Children were known to be especially fond of this oil as the mouth would turn black after eating it.

Nyagmaar – Oil was also extracted from black seeds known as *nyagmaar* bartered from the Monpas in exchange of fish, rice or yeast. The oil obtained from these seeds, however, was not used for internal consumption but was applied on the body for relief from body pain and aching joints.

NOTES AND REFERENCES

1. A lecture on the opening session of Gene Campaign's project *Indigenous Knowledge and Biodiversity* by Dr. Gupta, India International Centre, 7th July 2004.
2. *The Sherdukpens* by R.R.P. Sharma (1961), p. 9.

3. Ibid., p. 9.
4. See Religion for details.
5. *Tribes of Arunachal Pradesh in Transition* by Gurudas Das (1995), p. 86.
6. Ibid., pp. 87-88.
7. *Myths of NEFA* by Verrier Elwin (1958), Introduction, p. xiv.
8. Ibid., p. 3.
9. *Myths of NEFA* by Verrier Elwin (1958), pp. 3-4.
10. Ibid., p. 6.
11. See History for details.
12. I was informed that Kalakatang was earlier known as Chingy.
13. The river that flows by Rupa.
14. Migeji is a part of the Chao clan or the lower class among the Sherthukpens.

8

Material Culture

Before the establishment of markets and monetary economy, the Sherthukpens largely depended on an external supply of products of common need and comfort acquired through the practice of trade and barter. The Sherthukpens were skilled entrepreneurs who traded and bartered with most of their neighbours. With the gradual shift to monetary economy, the Sherthukpens started buying cheap readymade clothes. Today, they buy their necessary goods from the markets in Rupa and Shergaon. The emergence of markets provided easier access to goods and cheap substitutes began to replace a number of local Sherthukpen products. This, in turn, resulted in the withering of some of the indigenous crafts. Some of their arts and crafts are nearly extinct due to changes in their lifestyle and decreasing dependence on nature, as well as alternates and cheap substitutes available in the market. Nevertheless, some measures are being taken by the government for the revival of their ancient crafts.

Elwin observes in his *The Art of the NEFA* (1959),

> A great deal of tribal art is associated with religious beliefs and practices and as these weaken, the art weakens with them. Missionary influence has generally been highly destructive of folk art, whether it be dancing, song, carving or even weaving – for so many of these good things have been closely associated with 'pagan' ideas.

> Yet in spite of this the hill people, who love colour and beauty, have succeeded... in making many things that are original, striking and, in their own way, beautiful. They have an excellent taste in colour and in combining colours; some of them show remarkable skill in devising patterns and, if the old records are to be believed, they have developed many of today's designs during the past fifty years, and are still creating new patterns, partly under the stimulus of external example but largely as a result of their own natural zest for creation. The wood-carving often reveals vitality and strength; the cane-work reaches a high standard of technical perfection. In the art of personal adornment, even the remotest tribes reveal a singular fertility of invention.[1]

The Sherthukpen sense of aesthetics has undergone significant changes; and in the present day, the more prosperous enhance their homes with market goods and curios. On the other hand, the Crafts Centre at Bomdila has provided a platform for people to hone and better their skills as well as display the superlative samples of their art and craft. Though many of the tribes in Arunachal Pradesh, long isolated because of the geography and intertribal feuds, have only had minimal influence from the outside, the Sherthukpens, who, much like the Monpas, live in an area bordering both Tibet and Bhutan have been continually influenced and inspired by art emanating from both these countries—the common Lamaist heritage and the practice of trade and barter providing ample impetus for the same. Considerable influence has also been deciphered from the plains of Assam.

Elwin notes,

> All along the frontier Tibetan dress and ornaments may be seen, some of them imitated locally from trans-frontier models, others imported. Monpa painting is largely Tibetan in subject and technique. Nearer the plains the influence of the Assamese bazaars is no less evident, especially in the popularity of the Assamese endi silk.[2]

The lessening of superstition owing to the spread of education and awareness has also lifted many taboos associated with the production or use of material things which were a marked hindrance for artistic skill and proliferation. Today, many of the Sherthukpens do not restrict themselves to the traditional weaving of their forefathers but are more willing to experiment with other artistic traditions and produce handloom that is more applicable to their daily life. I met a young Sherthukpen girl in Rupa who is an expert weaver and was in the process of weaving a beautiful Naga shawl for the severe winter.

BASKETRY

Bamboo is abundant in the region and is an important raw material as it has a variety of uses. The Sherthukpen houses have a range of articles made of different types of bamboo and cane. Mats, baskets, mugs, fishing traps, baskets, bottle holders and containers, among other objects, are crafted by the people for self-consumption. Containers for the preparation, filtration and storage of beer are also made of bamboo. The few families not familiar with the art may purchase or barter the same from other households. Some of these articles can also be found in the nearby markets. Bamboo is easily obtained from the nearby forests but cane being rarer has to be brought from the neighbouring Khowas. It might be of some merit to examine the causes of the near extinction of cane from many of the forest areas, as the same situation prevailed in the Lepcha reserve of Dzongu in North Sikkim. Cane, once known to be aplenty, has nearly disappeared from the forest areas near the Lepcha settlements of Dzongu. The production of bamboo and the art associated with the plant should be put under special scanner not only in Arunachal but in the entire north-east, in light of the event of the flowering of Bamboo—synonymous to widespread devastation and infertility of land. Neither the government officials nor the Sherthukpens seemed either extremely aware or concerned about the prospects of such a phenomenon.

WEAVING

Weaving acquires special significance in tribal art and imagination. Many of the tribes of Arunachal Pradesh exhibit their age-old fascination and inquiry with the clatter of the loom in their imaginative mythology. A large number of myths originating from the region are focused on the origin and design of weaving. A Sherthukpen myth describes how a girl who is mocked by her peers because she cannot weave is redeemed by a snake who sometimes takes the form of a gallant youth. When he turns into a snake, he guides the dejected girl who copies the pattern of the snake skin and is able to produce the most exotic handloom beheld by her people.

Handlooms are widely distributed in Arunachal Pradesh and weaving is practised in almost every household. Weaving in the state is mainly a female task. They work on the simple loin-looms—the single-heddle tension loom and have also adopted the heavier looms of Assam. Sherthukpens weave textiles out of cotton thread which was brought from the plains, and also weave plant fibre.

Traditionally, the Sherthukpens rarely wove whole costumes as they mainly bartered cloth from the Kacharis. They are better known for weaving smaller articles of everyday use such as bags, knapsacks, etc. Angular geometrical patterns, lozenges, bands, stripes and fret patterns are common weaving patterns. The Sherthukpens weave the *bogre*, a bag worn over the shoulders that serves as a knapsack, which has a central motif of a right pointing swastika surrounded by lesser patters that may vary greatly. The colours used are mainly red, blue, black, green and yellow on a white or whitish background. *Bogre* is traditionally woven from the *hongchong* plant. The bark is soaked in boiling water and washed thoroughly after which the fibre is extracted and left to dry. Once dry, it is spun in spindles. The local yarn prepared from the plant *hongche* is extremely sturdy and used for making fishing nets. Sherthukpens also weave the colourful *daun*, a bag woven out of cotton threads. This is made on a smaller loom and the weaving is done with a shuttle. It is the only article that is produced for commercial purposes as it is very popular with the neighbouring tribes as well as the Kacharis. The tradition of weaving, however, has faced a setback with the easy availability of mill cloth and other readymade garments. A tendency to copy some of the designs of readymade cloths from the plains has been observed.

Elwin records the popular myth mentioned above connected to weaving,

> There was once an old woman who had two daughters. The elder daughter was very beautiful but nobody thought anything of her because she could not weave properly. The other girl made cloth with beautiful patterns but this girl could only weave plain cloth, and the other girls used to laugh at her.
>
> Once, when she was feeling very miserable about this, she did not eat all day and in the evening went down to bathe in the river. As she was bathing, a great snake came out of the water and she started to run away. But when the snake saw how beautiful she was, he turned into a handsome youth and said, 'Why are you frightened?' The girl replied, 'Because I thought you were a snake.' 'No! I'm not really a snake,' said the youth. 'I live beneath the water and I can take the form of a snake or a man as I please.' Then the girl, seeing the boy's beauty, came near him and they fell in love with one another. After that, every evening when the girl had eaten her supper, she used to go down secretly to the river and spend the night with her lover on the bank. Every morning the youth would turn into a snake and go down to his house beneath the water.
>
> One evening when they met as usual, the girl refused to speak, for she was very sad because she could not weave properly. After a lot of persuasion she told her lover about it and he said, 'Don't worry about this. In the morning I will come in my beautiful skin; you can take me to your house and when you sit at your loom, you can hold me in your lap and copy the patterns on my body.'
>
> The boy turned again into a snake and went into the water and girl sat all night on the river-bank. At dawn he came back as a snake in his beautiful skin. The girl took him home and sat down to her loom with him on her lap. The other girls came to watch but when they saw the snake, they ran away in fright. But soon she was making the finest cloth in the whole village.
>
> That evening the girl carried the snake down to the river-bank and he turned into a man again. In a few days the girl had made three beautiful pieces of cloth. She gave one to her sister, one to the other girls so that they could imitate it, and kept one for herself.
>
> After a little while, the snake said, 'This is no way to live. The right thing will be for me to marry you and take you to my house.' 'But how am I to live under the water?' asked the girl. 'Don't

worry about that.' He replied, 'I will come to you with a great party and many instruments of music and you will be able to live in the river quite happily.' So next morning the girl said to her mother, 'I am going to my husband.' 'What husband is this?' asked the mother. 'It is my snake-husband who taught me to weave.' 'But how can you do such a thing? He will kill you.' The mother alternatively abused and cajoled her, but she refused to listen.

After two days, the boy came with a great procession playing many instruments of music. To the eyes of the villagers, the visitors looked like snakes, but to the girl they looked like human beings. As her husband was taking her away, she said to her mother, 'I'm going now, but if ever you are in trouble come to the bank of the river and call me.' So the girl went into the river and deep down below the water there was a palace of gold and the two lived there happily and had many children.

Then one day her younger sister said, 'Why shouldn't I too marry a snake?' She went down to the river and found a hole where a black snake lived. She lay down beside it hoping that this snake also would turn into a handsome youth and marry her. But when he came out of his hole, he was just a snake and killed her.

Now the girl's mother had no one to look after her and she was very old; she could only hobble about and there was no food in the house. So one day she went weeping to the river-bank and cried, 'My daughter, my daughter!' Night fell and the girl came out of the water and said, 'Come with me.' Her mother refused, but her daughter tied a cloth round her face and dragged her down. There the old woman saw the palace of gold and a crowd of children crying, 'Granny.' They surrounded her, played with her dress and climbed into her lap. Suddenly they turned into snakes and coiled themselves round her. She threw them off in fright and they became human again.

After this the old woman said to her daughter, 'Send me home, this is too much for me.' Her son-in-law said, 'Very well, but I will give you something to take back with you.' He tied some sand in one piece of cloth and a little grain in another piece. He found a scrap of rope and a bit of wood each as long as his little finger. He tied these things up in a bundle and gave them to the old woman saying, 'Don't look at them on the way; take them home and put each of them in a separate basket as big as you can find. Then after a week open the baskets and see what you have.' Then he took her out of the water.

When she was left alone on the bank the old woman thought, 'I have been on a visit to the house of my daughter and son-in-law and they have given me no money but only these wretched things.' She felt so upset that she threw the bundle on the ground. But later she thought, 'Perhaps I had better do what my son-in-law said,' and she picked up all the things she could find and put them in little baskets. After a week she opened the baskets and found the bit of wood had turned into dried fish, the rope had turned into dried meat, the sand had become rice and the grain had become rice-seed. But since she had thrown away most of what her son-in-law had given her and had only put what was left in small baskets, there was not very much. But even then there was now something for her to eat and she lived on what she had until she died.[3]

CARPENTRY AND WOOD-CARVING

Traditionally, carpentry was not a specialised field and most households could produce the requisite woodwork themselves. Today, however, carpentry is more skilled and specialised and a number of Sherthukpens trained at the Bomdila cottage industries centre operate as carpenters in Rupa. Nonetheless, most Sherthukpens, especially those living at the rural fringes, can perform basic carpentry functions and can manufacture doors, tables, benches, boxes, cups and bowls to provide for their needs. Elwin's observations on the carpentry skills of the Sherthukpens (and the Monpas) are noted in *The Art of the NEFA* (1959). He writes,

> Both tribes are in their way good carpenters and produce doors, windows, boxes and wooden saddles. But their best work in wood is the manufacture of bowls, cups, plates and saucers, which are often beautifully done and are painted with a number of designs... An important stimulus to artistic creation is found in the Sherthukpen, Khamba and Monpa dances or pantomimes. These require ornate dresses and ornaments and large number of masks, some of which are so natural that they appear almost like real faces, while others represent birds and animals, and yet others are of what Maraini calls the protective horror type—ogres, men with twisted mouths, women with goitre—to drive away the spirits of evil.[4]

The pantomimes and dances performed by the Sherthukpens have acquired tremendous significance in the artistic traditions of these people and elaborate preparations are made to carry out these performances. Even the Thukpen Village Council has made statutory arrangements to ensure that the tradition receives ample patronage. The music and dance traditions of the Sherthukpens have been discussed in greater detail in the report.

SMITHY

The Sherthukpens of Jigaon, originally migrants from Bhutan, are known for their smithy skills in the region. They manufacture kitchen stoves, *daos*, knives, sickles, axes, etc. There is also a well-known silver smith family in the area which produces cups, *daos*, jewellery, trinkets, coins and pins. A Tibetan silver coin known as Betang is commonly used as raw material for jewellery and is obtained from the Monpa region of Tawang. This art form is, however, not indigenous to the Sherthukpens and is believed to have been another import from Bhutan. The silver goods were also sold in the neighbouring region as silversmiths were unavailable in the settlements of the Akas, Mijis and Khowas. Today, there are also a handful of Marwari silversmiths who have set up shops in Rupa.

BRIDGE-BUILDING

Bridge-building never really evolved into a fine art with the Sherthukpens. The bridges made by them remain rather crude and unsophisticated. However, they are functional and can be spotted even in the remote areas of the Sherthukpen belt. Bridges are constructed by the simple principle of aligning sturdy wooden planks over a body of water and then covering the vertical logs with smaller planks that are interlocked and secured. Sometimes the vertical logs are provided additional support by aligning an extra plank to support the middle section of the bridge.

HUNTING

Sherthukpens are expert hunters and have a number of indigenous methods to hunt game. Hunting can be both a pastime and a necessity, especially for the poor people in the villages in the harsh winter months when the fields are barren

Phak is of a mildly sweet flavour and is prepared by fermented maize or rice left for a period of about 10 days.

The maize based *phak* is the most popular drink of the Sherthukpens and is prepared in almost every rural or urban household on a regular basis. Maize is pounded and boiled in a large copper pot. When the maize is half done the pot is lifted off the fire and left to cool. It is then mixed with ground rice and yeast brought from the market, or *sangkhya*, a wild herb used as a fermenting agent. This is mixed well with the cooling maize, transferred into a bamboo container and left undisturbed for a week or more. A portion of the fermented mix is used to prepare *phak* for daily consumption. The mix is put into a snaky, malleable cane bag called *thok* and squeezed thoroughly. The liquid is collected, heated and added with some hot water and then served.

Arah is the alcoholic distilled drink of the Sherthukpens. The fermented maize or rice is put through a distillation process in which the fermented mix is heated with water on fire in a metal container closed with a tight lid which is attached to a pipe linked to a smaller container kept on the floor. The mix is heated over fire. Slowly the evaporated water and alcoholic content emanating from the boiling mix turns into vapour and gathers on the inside of the lid. A cooling process is generated by placing cold water over the lid which is replaced from time to time and helps in the condensation of the vapour in the boiling container. The distilled vapour, when condensed rolls down the pipe attached to the small container on the floor. This is the distilled clear drink of *arah* which is mixed with water and consumed on occasions by the Sherthukpens.

Sherthukpens have also taken to drinking alcoholic beverages and beer from outside. Alcoholic drinks brought from the market are served in the region even during ceremonial functions, as an increasing number of men and women are abandoning the local beverages in favour of the drinks available in the market.

NOTES AND REFERENCES

1. *The Sherdukpens* by R.R.P. Sharma (1961), p. 37.
2. Gaur or *Bos frontalis.*

11

Music and Dance

Festivals, music and dance comprise the most important recreational activities of the Sherthukpens. Festivals are occasions for artistic performances and, besides recreation, Sherthukpens also ascribe certain moral and ethical values to their music and dance traditions—perhaps a later influence of the Lamaist ideology and practice. However, today this facet is well ingrained in their culture and ideology. Traditionally, besides festivals, music and dance, there were no other organised means of revelry that brought the whole community together. Today, events like cricket and football matches, and youth festivals also attract people on a large scale.

During my time in Rupa, there was a cricket tournament organised between Bomdila and Rupa. The event was well attended by the people of Rupa and there were some stalls put up for food and games to attract a larger crowd. Tambola was played, especially by the not-so-interested-in-cricket womenfolk and a palpable influence of the neighbouring Army cantonment in the organisation of the entire affair was observed. There are also some snooker outlets in Rupa and the game is gaining increasing popularity among the young men who sometimes spend their entire days in these outlets during the winter months. This reflects a change in the recreational activities of the Sherthukpens. However, such activities and events yet do not have the potential to draw people from the rural areas in large numbers.

Another game which is gaining more popularity than snooker, and is played by both men and women, is card gambling. It is a common sight to see groups of men huddled together for hours, concentrating on a bunch of cards. The well-off women in Rupa organise teams for playing cards and meet in one of their homes during the afternoon. I was told by one of the players that they could lose an average of Rs. 700 a day on the game. Nevertheless, none of these recreational activities have managed to inspire and summon Sherthukpens like their age-old festivals, and music and dance traditions. During events like the *Khiksaba*, entire villages come and camp in Rupa to participate in the celebrations of the festival which is solemnised with the performance of a number of traditional songs and dances.

The musical traditions and interests of the Sherthukpens have been somewhat influenced and altered by outsiders. Tibetan music has a marked influence on what is today perceived as Sherthukpen music. Hindi film music is becoming increasingly popular as well. Younger Sherthukpens, especially in the better connected areas, are perhaps more familiar with Bollywood music today, than with their traditional songs.

MUSIC

The traditional songs or *hun* of the Sherthukpens are sung on various occasions. Sherthukpen songs are mainly dedicated to four emotions: love, comedy, tragedy and ceremony. The Sherthukpen musical tradition could be classified into songs sung during marriage ceremonies, romantic songs, welcome and farewell songs, and songs sung during childbirth, hunting, fishing, and honey collection as well as songs sung while performing agricultural processes, especially during harvest time. Their musical tradition is believed to have been considerably influenced by Tibetan music and pitch. There is no fixed time for their rendering. Indeed, any occasion when a few Sherthukpens get together for work or pleasure may be considered a fit occasion for their favourite pastime. People can often be found singing along while performing their chores like sowing, weeding, constructing houses or simply enjoying a peaceful moment sitting around the bonfire. However, songs are most frequently sung on occasions like marriages, birth and after the harvest.

The Sherthukpens traditionally sing only one song during honey collection. The song is a request to the bees to grant the Sherthukpens their honey and is only sung by men.

We are not Indians, nor Tibetans, Bhutanese or Akas.
We are the people of Lama Tampie Dreama
We have come to take the honey from you, so that
The honey may be put in a brompu
And the Lama may bless people from the prasad.

According to the information obtained from the people in the Sherthukpen belt, their ancestors have been long familiar with the bamboo flute. However, it is unclear whether the Sherthukpens were the first to play the instrument or had learnt the art of playing the flute from some of their neighbours. There are also two variations of a simple instrument known as *orang* that was traditionally played by the Sherthukpens. Both *orangs* were hand-held instruments that were played by striking the tongue repeatedly with a thread.

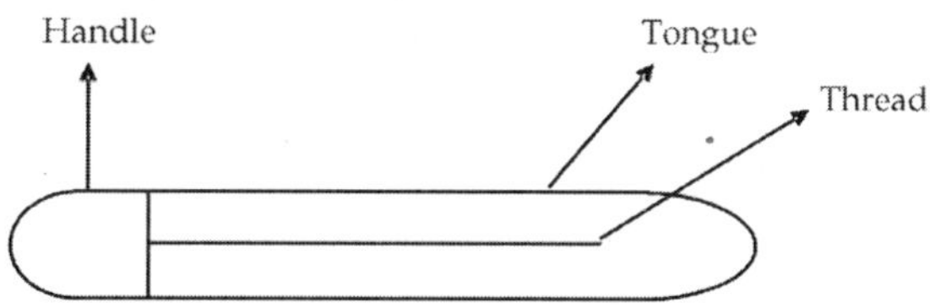

DANCE

The Sherthukpens are known throughout the region for their dancing and pantomime tradition. They have a befitting dance for almost every occasion. They have a dance for the theme of love, war, theft, rainfall, nature and also one to seek children. They have dances dedicated to myriad birds and animals like the yak dance, deer dance, eagle dance, hare dance, snake dance, pig, god, tiger, monkey, cow, rat and even pig dance. These dances are performed with elaborate painted masks traditionally procured from the Lamaist centres of Tawang and Dirang.

Elwin describes the lore on which the deer dance is based.

> Long ago, when Apapek and his three sons were living together, the old man took his eldest and youngest sons to the forest to hunt. They saw a deer and their dog chased it round and round in a circle and Apapek shot it with a poisoned arrow. But the poison did not kill the deer; it only made it drunk with a kind of madness. Apapek and his sons tried to catch but it danced among them; it did not run away or fall down and die, but simply went on dancing.
>
> This went on for a long time until Chungba-Sangyat came to them and said, 'Don't kill this deer, but let it go.' Apapek said 'But I have already shot it and there is poison in its body. How can we let it go?' Chungba-Sangyat said, 'Even so, let it go, for it would be a sin to eat its flesh.' The boys agreed but Apapek said, 'I don't know anything about sin. I am an old man now and am hungry for meat, so whether you like it or not, I am going to eat it.' But Chungba-Sangyat still refused to let him do this and since Apapek continued to demand the meat, he removed the poison from the deer's body and it ran away.[1]

These dances are remarkably similar to the ones performed by the Monpas who are also the followers of Lamaism. The Sherthukpens have some indigenous dances but these are not as well established as the ones mentioned above because these received Lamaist patronage, while the indigenous dances perished in the light of the benefaction given to anything Lamaist and, therefore, considered more refined and genteel than traditions that had sprung from their original animist faith. The dances are mainly performed by men and the Sherthukpens have specialised dancers or *chhampo,* dance troupe, who dedicate their time to the art. There are mainly two *chhampos* that are maintained by the Sherthukpens—the Ajilamu and yak dance troupes.

Many of the dances have specific moral values attached to them and the ethos of not killing or sacrificing animals is an oft-repeated theme in many of the Sherthukpen dances. The hunter dance, also known as the *Bardu Chaam*, depicts the story of what happens to a hunter after he dies. The dance is performed by dancers dressed up as the twelve animals of the Tibetan horoscope—rat, ox, tiger, hare, dragon, snake, horse, sheep, monkey, cock, dog, and hog. The hunter goes to hell after his death, which according to the prevailing morality is a direct consequence of hunting and killing animals. In hell, the hunter is tortured by the animals he had killed in his lifetime. However, unlike on the earth, the animals are strong and united and the hunter is no match for the united front of the animals and is, thus, befittingly punished for his sins.

The most important dance of the Sherthukpens is the pantomime of Ajilamu, which is based on a famous Sherthukpen myth recorded by Verrier Elwin.[2] The dance is performed by five men; one plays the part of the king, two are dressed up as demons and two as queens. There are two more people who do not participate in the dance but play the drum and cymbals. Curiously, this pantomime has marked parallels to the *Ramayana* and no one today is aware of the beginnings of this traditional dance. However, since it is a traditional dance and commands significance in the Sherthukpen culture, the dance continues to be performed.

According to the myth, once upon a time, the king of Lhasa called Chajernurjan had two beautiful wives with the names of Luma and Lame. The demons saw the queens taking a bath and so enticed were they by their beauty that they kidnapped Lamu and Lame and carried them away to their abode. The king, greatly disturbed by the disappearance of his two wives, set out to look for them. He finally found them in the home of the demons Nyapa and Nyaro and asked them what had transpired, in a secret language. The queens replied singing in the same language and told the king about their plight. On learning that his queens were kidnapped, the king got furious and asked the demons to release the queens or face his wrath. The demons, frightened by the outburst and might of the king, readily released the queens and requested the king to pardon them. The magnanimous king forgave the demons and they all danced together with the queens.

NOTES AND REFERENCES

1. *Myths of the North-East Frontier of India* by Verrier Elwin (1958), p. 376. This is the story behind the Sherdukpen Deer Dance, which is performed with great vigour by a man wearing a mask which represents a deer's head with spreading antlers.
2. *Myths of the North-East Frontier of India* by Verrier Elwin (1958), pp. 122-23.

12

Behaviour and Morality

The internal structure of the tribal societies in Arunachal was not as egalitarian as is often projected. A distinct inequality among the people was prevalent even during the time when people subsisted only on *jhum* cultivation. Practices like slavery and headhunting were not uncommon, and peace was often juxtaposed with bloody inter-tribal feuds. However, almost every early account on the hill tribes of Arunachal, while detailing the people as war-like in their disposition, makes an exception for the 'Buddhist tribes'. The Sherthukpens, with the Monpas, have been long known for their characteristic sense of harmony, and are referred to as friendly and mild mannered. However, the Sherthukpens have been known to indulge in warfare as well. The imposition of the *posa* by the British is a testimony to such acts and so is a *chorten* in Rupa that stands as a symbol of repentance for once killing a large number of Kacharis.

Here, the construction of the *chorten* reveals some interesting characteristics about the Sherthukpens. It symbolises the acceptance of having sinned, and emphasises the emotion of repentance. These moral standpoints are commonly interpreted as the influence of Lamaism on an unruly people who were gradually softened by the religion. Such an assumption might hold true, had the Sherthukpens been under the sway of Lamaism since the ancient times. However, as already discussed, Lamaism became a dominant force in Rupa only in the 60s and even today a sizable number of Sherthukpens practise Lamaism only marginally. It is indeed difficult to ascertain whether the morality and behaviour of a strict follower of Lamaism is distinct from that of a lay Sherthukpen. While the head Lama of the Rupa monastery, Lama Yeshi Tenzing, might think so, I could find no such variations during my fieldwork and no local to champion the Lama's claims.[1] The only significant variation that may be made along the lines of religion is that Lamaism is relatively more prominent among the rich as compared to the poor.

It is perhaps of significance to ask what led to the generalisations on the behavioural patterns of the Sherthukpens. Why have they always been clubbed together with the Monpas and other 'Buddhist' tribes? After all, Lamaism was adopted by the Monpas much earlier than the Sherthukpens. Could it be that the Sherthukpens, being a smaller tribe in their immediate vicinity, were under a marked influence of the Monpas and imbibed their sense of morality much before they formally accepted their religion? Were the Sherthukpens awestruck by the grand Lamasery at Tawang, and realised they had nothing to equal it?[2] Were they humbled by the 'refined' culture imported from Tibet and by their organised holy men who stood out in their fine maroon and yellow robes?[3] These speculations might be hard to establish but it is clear that many among those who exerted substantial influence among the Sherthukpens patronised Lamaism and encouraged the people to follow suit as well.[4] However, with the available information and research, it is difficult to say that such a transition could have resulted in a shift in the behavioural patterns of the people. Indeed, if such a claim is held true then the behaviour and morality of the people of Rupa should be distinct from that of those living in villages like Gorwa or Membachur.[5] It might be possible to find such discrepancies, but these are a result of the urban-rural divide rather than the outcome of religious beliefs and practices. Hence, I am unable to support the claims made by my predecessors that the behaviour and morality of the Sherthukpens is largely the result of the adoption of Lamaism, or Tibetan Buddhism.

I shall further endeavour to detail the same, purely on the basis of my research and field study. I found the Sherthukpens to be immensely cordial, friendly and mild-mannered. This is because in known history, the Sherthukpens were never an isolated people. For long, they have been known to interact with outsiders for the purpose of barter and trade. They have also played the role of active middlemen in the trade between Tibet and Assam and were frequent travellers on the ancient trade route that linked the two regions. Much of the tribes in Arunachal did not enjoy such access and interaction with other communities. Such an interaction is bound to have had an impact on the Sherthukpen psyche, making them more approachable to outsiders. This could have led to their being referred to as friendly whenever an outsider came in contact with them.

Another distinct trait that throws light on the point made above is that I found the people to be highly tolerant of other faiths and ideologies. This is especially true for Rupa, which has the largest population of non-Sherthukpens in the region. I was repeatedly told that the Sherthukpens in Rupa celebrate all festivals, with other communities, be it Diwali, Id or Christmas. They share cordial relations with the other minorities living in Rupa and there appears to be no marked discord among them. The Sherthukpens, long used to trading relations with outsiders, have been further influenced by the developments after the amalgam with India. Many of the Sherthukpens in Rupa, now in their twenties and thirties, went to the school in town that was run by Hindu missions. The morning prayers recited by these children are reminiscent of the *aartis* sung in temples that eulogise secular traditions. It would not be out of line to say that the Sherthukpens in Rupa are more comfortable with Hinduism represented by the Marwaris and Nepalis in town as compared to Christianity brought to town on a regular basis by guitar sporting youths from Nagaland who do not speak Hindi. However, the discomfort for Christianity is not owing to the religion itself but to the practice of conversion. While the Sherthukpens might feel threatened by the growing number of converts to

Christianity, they do not perceive the same threat from the Hindu missions. The chain of Vivekananda Schools, known for imparting high quality education in the state, has also helped forge greater understanding among the people for Hinduism.

Jest forms an important part of the lives of the Sherthukpens and much energy and time is spent on entertainment, which is almost always coupled with consuming a fair amount of food and drink. Sherthukpens are fun-loving and seldom look for special occasions for revelry and even the smallest occasion is a reason to celebrate. The evening I reached Doimara, a group of young men from Shergaon were in the village to play a cricket match in the foothills. The villagers gathered to celebrate the event in the evening and sang and danced over cupfuls of *phak* till late in the night. My visit to some villages resulted in similar revelry as well.

Emotional outbursts are rare and, except for the young people exposed to media, they are seldom known to dramatise their emotions. Speech has great importance and an eloquent speaker is highly esteemed in the community. Any display of anger or aggression is discouraged and rash and emotional outbursts are almost always met with vehement disapproval. However, some Thongs can be rather arrogant while dealing with people less privileged than themselves. Even so, amity commonly prevails and the Thongs and Chaos share reasonably cordial relations.

Sherthukpens do not like being ordered around. However, they are usually obedient and do not easily defy a superior if the basic decorum is maintained. They have deference for authority and seek social approval in their endeavours. There is regard for the wisdom of the aged and indulgence in the playfulness of children. Young people are rarely discourteous. Children are brought up to respect not only the elders but also the institutions and ideologies esteemed by them. Any display of discourtesy is instantly put down. In spite of often living with families with young children, I do not recollect a Sherthukpen child being impolite. Children, if it might be said, are more seen than heard. I found them to be timid, shy, cheerful, extremely polite and well behaved. Was there a lack of individualism in their demeanour? Or, is it that the sentiment attached to individualism by the 'mainstream', more often than not, tends to be a display of irreverence, aggression and discontentment with the larger family or community?

Some commonly used synonyms for individualism are uniqueness, egoism, individuality, independence, distinctiveness, eccentricity and selfishness. The Oxford dictionary defines individuality as "the quality or character of a person or thing that makes them different from others." Individualism among Sherthukpens does not seem to be as suppressed as, say, among the Lepchas of Dzongu. However, the characteristic is not typically encouraged among the Sherthukpens and sanctions are granted to behaviour types that bind the community-life ethos. Gorer in the 1930s made some interesting observations on the initial life of Lepcha babies, which he linked to their lack of individualism.

> From the point of view of physical well-being, Lepcha babies appear to experience the minimum of frustration and therefore it would seem that in the first few months of life there are few experiences to evoke aggression. But parallel with this gratification of physiological appetites, there is the considerable physical restrain which the babies endure through passing the majority of their waking hours firmly tied to the back of their guardian, and also the complete lack of encouragement which their elders give to their babies' earlier self-maximating activities and attempts to acquire body techniques and physical independence. Young babies get no social approval from their attempts to crawl and walk...[6]

This observation is of relevance here. Sherthukpen children receive much the same treatment in their initial years; however, the people do not reveal similar behaviour types. The discernable lack of competition and individualism among the Lepchas is not as evident among the Sherthukpens who have been known to be active middlemen and possess relatively keen business skills. There are also a number of budding entrepreneurs in the Sherthukpen region.[7]

For the first three years, a Sherthukpen child receives constant attention and care. Fastened to his mother's back, a child accompanies her everywhere. The next couple of years are spent mainly in the company of playmates. There are no cares, and days are spent in joyful abandon, running and playing around with friends. During this period, the parents allow a child to roam freely and the restriction of movement experienced in the early years is not imposed any longer as long as he eats and sleeps well. The freedom of a troublesome or impolite child, however, may be curtailed sufficiently. This leads us to believe that individualism may not be discouraged unless it comes in conflict with communal mores.

Around the age of eight, a child is considered more responsible and assigned some household chores and duties. He/she is expected to help at home, take care of younger siblings and assist the parents in agricultural activities. School-going children are expected to return from school and accomplish their chores. During this age, children tend to stay with people of the same sex; girls stay at home with their mothers or play with other girls in the village, and boys help their fathers in the fields and forests. The segregation of sexes is, however, not imposed and a fair bit of interaction with children of the opposite sex also takes place. Personal appearance is important to the Sherthukpens and this characteristic is also highlighted in their lore. Sherthukpens give significant attention to their appearance, especially during adolescence. They accomplish tasks allocated to them at home and largely mingle with a group of close friends. They are shy of interacting with people of the opposite sex in public. In time, they join a specific dormitory which opens the way for socialisation and understanding with the opposite sex.[8]

The larger community is extremely important to the Sherthukpens and forms the bedrock of their identity. A Sherthukpen grows up defining himself as a part of the community rather than a specific individual. Sherthukpens, in my observation, find it difficult to be alone. When left all by themselves, they will almost always try to seek company. Nonetheless, Sherthukpens are highly sensitive about intruding and can interpret and respect the need for space and independence in others as long as a person carries out his/her social obligations. Even many among the well-to-do, who often live outside of the Sherthukpen belt, cannot imagine settling down elsewhere. The ex-CM R.K. Krimey, who was in power for a number of terms, has built a gargantuan fortress-like house in Rupa. This is so even though many people openly declare that his house is made from the money of the common people and that he is extremely corrupt. However, few Sherthukpens would attempt direct abuse or hostility because they respect hierarchy and see the merit in maintaining the *status quo*. The regard that people express for the Thukpen Village Council (TVC), already discussed in the report, emphasises their reverence to their system of indigenous command.[9] I met a number of people in the rural fringes who expressed their resentment with the TVC. It was interesting to note that in spite of the grave nature of the allegations—favouritism, corruption, centralisation of power and high-handedness—the manner in which they were made was almost apologetic. This is so in spite of, and because of, the glaring inequality that persists within the social organisation of the Sherthukpens.

Crime is rare. Nevertheless, when it does take place, the people are by and large forgiving. Sherthukpens are of the opinion that once a culprit repents for his crime and is willing to endure the punishment given to him, he should be forgiven. They do not like to carry a grudge for too long. People tend to avoid confrontations and try to resolve problems and disputes in a peaceful manner. I heard a story of two notorious brothers, Singji and Mazak, that took place about 40 years ago. They were born of an Assamese tribal father who married a Chao girl and they settled in Rupa. Their two sons were extremely mischievous and lost few opportunities to create a stir in town. One day they decided to steal someone's cow and sold it in the market. The villagers, tired of their repeated misdemeanours, decided to punish them. They were locked up in the *dukang*, a dark cell for jailing miscreants, for three days without food. It is said that the two brothers managed to break out of the *dukang* and after they came out, they realised that the people would be even more furious with them. They were petrified of the prospects of staying back, as breaking the jail is an extremely serious crime, and ran away to the plains. They returned after

seven or eight years and decided to redeem themselves. After their return, they exhibited good citizenry and participated in all community activities. The Sherthukpens too forgave them for the past. Mazak died a few years ago of old age. Sinji is still alive, and often performs voluntary work for the community and is well liked by everyone, especially the older Sherthukpens who remember his early days.

Sherthukpens can be lazy and completely prescribe to the oblivion of intoxicants like *phak* and alcohol. Many people are happy to produce enough to subsist and would rather spend the rest of their time in more entertaining activities than toiling away for surplus. However, with the growing economic disparity between the urban and rural, rich and poor, on the one hand, and the opening prospects of progress on the other, such dynamics are gradually changing. There is also a growing awareness among the rural and poor to educate their children.

The sanctions and taboos prescribed by their system of faith are deemed sacrosanct. Sherthukpens can be highly superstitious and a large number of them tend to subscribe to supernatural cures, especially when confronted with ill-health. Even today the *dzizi* is frequently summoned to cure illnesses. I spoke to a number of educated people who all claimed that they had witnessed a *dzizi* miraculously cure many people of acute sicknesses. The Senior Medical Officer at Rupa, Dr. T. Lhamu, said that many patients only come to a doctor when the *dzizi's* ceremonies fail to yield the desired result. Often, by this time, the patient's health has deteriorated significantly and if the patient does not recover, they blame it on the doctor and Western medicine. She also said that while the level of hygiene in Rupa was satisfactory, the people living in the villages and hamlets had to be made more aware of better hygiene and cleanliness. Indeed, ablutions, especially in the villages, remain infrequent, if not rare. However, people buy and use cleaning agents like soaps and detergents from the nearby markets and shops.

GENDER

The Sherthukpen social order is patriarchal. The head of a Sherthukpen family is male. *Gaonburahs* are almost always male and all other important indigenous positions of command and decision-making are bestowed on men. Even so, the presence of a woman in the family and community is highly valued and so is her productive capacity. Sherthukpen women work extremely hard and, in fact for longer hours than men. Almost all the household chores—drawing water, cooking, cleaning, washing, taking care of the young, animal care, brewing of alcoholic drinks, etc.—are accomplished by women. Weaving, spinning and knitting are also performed mainly by women. They also work in the fields and perform other agricultural activities. The only tasks that are purely accomplished by men among the Sherthukpens are ploughing, felling of trees, honey collection, hunting and fishing. Sherthukpen women have a quiet efficiency about them. They are highly dextrous and manage to accomplish their daily chores with minimum fuss. Almost all the women, especially in the villages, weave. It is an essential part of the grooming of a woman. However, men may at times accomplish the duties commonly performed by women. I witnessed a number of men helping their wives or daughters in the household chores. Men, however, are not bound to do so and some of them feel little need to be of help, and spend their time idling with their mates and peer groups.

The daughter cannot inherit any landed property from the father, although exceptions exist, and her standing in her original family is somewhat diminished after she is married off. However, the Sherthukpen woman leads a reasonably democratic existence, and participates in the social, economic and decision-making processes of her immediate family and society.

Thong men occupy the highest platform during *Khiksaba* while the Chaos and women sit below them. As already discussed, in the religious domain a Sherthukpen woman seems to be much inferior to her male counterpart.[10]

A number of old women in the Sherthukpen region said that the quality they most cherish in a daughter-in-law is hard work. A lazy girl is least desired. Other considerations are the reputation and clan of the girl's family; and finally, the son's wish. Sherthukpen women, like the men, seek social approval in their endeavours. The dignity of the family and clan has to be upheld and women are hesitant to jeopardise the existing dynamics. The mores and laws of the land pertaining to marriage favour tribal endogamy and can be somewhat insular. This makes many women suspicious of men who are non-Sherthukpen. It is interesting to note that in many cases of Sherthukpen women marrying men from outside, the men often settle within the Sherthukpen area. This adds much to her sense of security, as most of the women seem to fear the prospect of living far away from their region. In times of crisis, they not only look upon their immediate family for help but can also address the larger social structure for security and protection.

Observing the system of marriage among the Sherthukpens elucidates some interesting aspects of a woman's social standing. According to the Sherthukpen tradition, the gift of a yak and sheep is the fixed bride price. The yak and sheep are traditionally said to be bartered for the girl and thus, the bride does not partake of the meat of the animals paid as bride price. This illustrates that marriage is conducted on the principle of exchange and did not evolve on a philosophy that was far removed from their trading practices. Is it legitimate to deduce that the daughter was a mere commodity? Perhaps not; while this observation might hold true for some other tribes in Arunachal like the Akas and Mijis who are polygamous and can purchase as many wives as they like, provided they can pay the requisite number of *mithuns*, the same is not true among the Sherthukpens. The point of difference is that unlike the Akas, the Sherthukpens are strictly monogamous and hence the value of a wife is not that of a mere commodity but may be comparable to a valuable that may be purchased only once in a lifetime. This difference automatically enhances the status of a Sherthukpen woman *vis-à-vis* the polygamous tribes in the region. During a marriage ceremony, the *dochdo*, or orator, rises and outlines the universality of marriage, saying that girls have to ultimately marry and go and live in the husband's house. The father then tells his daughter that he has made a bargain in which he has lost his daughter, and blesses her. This elucidates that though marriage is a transaction, it is a deal which has been struck because of its unavoidable nature. Moreover, the father confesses to having suffered a grave loss in the transaction and publicly expresses his anguish.

Domestic violence is not common among the Sherthukpens. The family I was staying with, in Rupa, told me that there was a Bengali man in government service who had rented a room in their house. His wife came to stay with him during the summer. I was told that the family was shocked to find the seemingly subdued Bengali gentleman to be a regular wife-beater. Tired of the nightly scuffle, the landlady eventually decided to intervene. One evening she entered their room to find the man pulling his wife's hair and hitting her with a stick as she lay sobbing on the floor. The landlady was so aghast at the sight that she could barely get the words out of her mouth. She told me that even Sherthukpen couples sometimes fight but not in this manner, "Our men are not so insensitive, and if they were then our women simply won't take it. They would hit them back." She said that no conjugal relationship was worth such humiliation for a woman.

Ironically, in a society that does not encourage violence against women, the Sherthukpen administration had a highly archaic custom of dealing with unmarried women impregnated by non-Sherthukpens. They would first press her to reveal the name of the child's father. If she divulged the information and the man in question agreed on having had intimate relations with the girl, they would be asked to marry. However, owing to circumstances, if such a marriage could not take place, the woman was tied to a post in the grounds of the monastery. Once secured to the post, she received 108 lashes by the young men of the community. The rationale for not severely punishing the man, according to indigenous law, is that unless the woman is punished, the name of the father will not be revealed and the child might have to be 'illegitimate' throughout his life. It must be mentioned that there is a strong social taboo in the Sherthukpen society against illegitimate children.[11]

The status of a woman is enhanced after she is married even though parents do not commonly perceive a girl to be a burden and seldom put undue pressure on girls to get married.

The status of both the husband and wife is believed to be enhanced by the birth of an offspring. The presence of a son in a Sherthukpen family is essential, as the daughters are not allowed to inherit property. The birth of a boy is more esteemed than that of a girl and sons may, at times, be overindulged and spoiled by the family. Stress is laid upon the 'correct' upbringing of a girl child and girls are made to spend more time at home or with their parents. Even so, women lead a fairly free life and assert their views and independence within their domain. They do not seem to take kindly to overbearing male dominion.

NOTES AND REFERENCES

1. This aspect has been discussed in the chapter Religion in greater detail.
2. The Tawang monastery was under its mother monastery of Drepung, in Tibet. Fürer-Haimendorf notes that the Monpas showed a preference for the British rule. It was earlier assumed that they were migrants from Tibet. Later, it was known that the Monpas were immigrants not from Tibet but Bhutan. This might perhaps be the rationale as to why the Monpas accepted the McMohan line rather ungrudgingly.
3. The Tawang area was under Tibetan rule till the 60s, and Tibet and its culture was highly esteemed among the people living in Western Arunachal. These included the Sherthukpens as well, who shared trade and barter relations with Tibet; and the goods bartered from the Tibetans were in great demand by the people. Some of the rich are believed to have dressed in Tibetan finery as well.
4. See Religion for details.
5. Lamaism is most dominant in Rupa and least in remote villages like Gorwa where the sway of the Lo is more widespread.
6. *The Lepchas of Sikkim* by Geoffrey Gorer (1987), p. 450.
7. See Economy for details.
8. See Marriage in Social Organisation for details of the dormitory system.
9. See Socio-Political System for details.
10. See Religion for greater exploration on the role of women within the religious folds.
11. For details on marriage with outsiders, please see the footnotes of Thukpen Village Council, Socio-Political System.

13

Modernity and Change

The Sherthukpens, and other tribes inhabiting Arunachal Pradesh were tucked away in a mountainous landscape not easily reachable from the low lying plains, and as a result, isolated from much of the country. People lived here for centuries as prescribed by the law of the land established by their chiefs and forefathers. Influences and contacts with outsiders were limited and did not impress themselves substantially on the indigenous life and people. As a result, not much changed in this highland region for centuries. The Ahoms and the British largely left the hill tribes alone. The initial contacts were often hostile and only a minimum interaction was initiated by the rulers to keep a check on the tribals from assaulting and carrying away their lesser subjects.

Things changed after the 1962 Sino-India border conflict. The Himalayan state that was known to most Indians only by its snowbound passes and the virtue of it being the first to receive the morning sun was carved with long stretches of roads and studded with administrative offices. Townships grew and spread, new districts developed and the relentless Border Roads Organisation helped connect forgotten Arunachal to what is vaguely termed as 'the great Indian mainstream'. Arunachal Pradesh's strategic importance was too great to be left to its own devices.

The ideology of the Indian Administration witnessed a decisive shift from the Nehru-Elwin Policy[1] of tribal revivalism and protectionism to a policy of integration, immediately after the Sino-Indian border conflict. This radical change in perspective was pursued aggressively after 1972. NEFA was declared a Union Territory of India under the new name of Arunachal Pradesh in 1972. The first election to the Legislative Assembly was held in 1980, which paved the way for party line politics. The restructuring carried on till it was significantly consolidated in 1987 and the Union Territory of Arunachal Pradesh was granted statehood. English and Hindi were pursued in schools and added thrust was given towards popularising Hindi and Hindu missions.

The state, along with the Centre, has launched various development schemes and programmes to uplift the standard of living of the Sherthukpens, and enabled them to be a greater part of the Indian mainstream. Government-sponsored schemes in the field of education, health, economy, agriculture and animal husbandry, among others, have been successfully implemented. Given the nature of remoteness of the region, this endeavour has not been a simple one and a lot yet remains to be accomplished. It must be mentioned that the topography and distribution of population across this beautiful yet formidable region makes it difficult for people living away from the semi-urban settlements to access the facilities now available to the people.

The neighbouring army settlement in Rupa provided another catalyst to change. Many Sherthukpens, however, regret granting their land to the army today owing to a measure of forcefulness displayed by the army on occasions. The interaction between the army and the Sherthukpens is limited. Soldiers come to the market in Rupa for their necessities and the Sherthukpens with some contacts in the army try to purchase goods from the canteen. The army also extends help if there is a disruption in the telephone lines and other civil amenities in Rupa. Nevertheless, there is a palpable mistrust among the Sherthukpens for the army. This could be the result of a rape that is reported to have taken place in Rupa some years ago. The man in question was a soldier. The Sherthukpen women are discouraged from interacting with plainsmen and especially soldiers because they are of the opinion that girls from the North-East are perceived as easy and characterless by the mainstream. Certain influences, however, have filtered down in spite of the prevailing mistrust. The organisation of the cricket match with food and games' stalls and sessions of Tombola, already discussed in the report, is an example.[2]

The musical traditions and interests of the Sherthukpens have been somewhat influenced and altered by outsiders. Hindi film music is becoming increasingly popular. Young Sherthukpens, especially in the better-connected areas, are more familiar with Bollywood music today, than with their traditional songs. Television too has resulted in a marked influence. The *saas-bahu* serials are extremely popular among the womenfolk in the semi-urban settlements while the younger people swear by the music and movie channels. A girl said that, "We watch TV and learn a lot from it. We try to copy the styles and clothes and that is how we know what is fashionable in the big cities." Unfortunately, the world depicted in Hindi TV soaps is perceived as a representation of the mainstream reality by the Sherthukpens, much like the manner in which the Indian mainstream sees the West purely through Hollywood films and Western soaps on TV.

Most Sherthukpens do not have a strong opinion on Chinese claims to the territory. Their local affiliations with the Kacharis and Assam have insured that they have little in common with the Chinese. The ambivalence on the part of some prominent citizens of Arunachal, as far as the Sherthukpens are concerned, is a political gimmick. The question of granting greater rights to the refugees in Arunachal, however, draws some strong reactions from the more literate Sherthukpens. They unanimously and vehemently disagree on having to share their land and wealth with outsiders.

The Akas and Mijis proved to be a source of terror and disruption for the Sherthukpens well up to the 1940s, but such assaults changed in both frequency and intensity. After Bomdila, the settlements of Rupa and Shergaon developed into townships. At present, Rupa is the Sub-Divisional Headquarters and Shergaon the C.O. Headquarters in the district. The 2001 census report in the Rupa Circle records a total population of 9,450 people with 5,767 males and 3,683 females. The number of females per 1,000 males is 749 (district level). The decennial growth rate at the district level is + 32.21. Health, education and development centres have been set up in the Sherthukpen region and roads are being built to connect areas that remain isolated. There is a Community Health Centre in Rupa and sub-centres in Shergaon, Morshing, Jigaon and Mukuthing. The nearest college from the Sherthukpen belt is at Bomdila as there are no colleges yet in the region. Development schemes are being implemented but a lot more needs to be accomplished, especially in the field of health and education. The government-run health outpost in Rupa is underequipped. The senior medical officer Dr. T. Lhamu informed me that the health centre is only equipped for clinical checkups. There is no lab and not even an X-ray machine in the hospital. People have to travel all the way to Bomdila for more thorough checkups. The doctor said that there is a regular shortage of medicines in the health centre as well.

In the field of agriculture, the Agriculture Development officer S.C. Khrimey listed the following schemes that have been launched by the government: macro management scheme, land development, HYV seed programme, fertilizer and nutrient management, tools and implements programme, self-employment schemes for educated unemployed youth, national watershed development under rain-fed areas, national watershed development under shifting cultivation areas, and seed supply under CCS 100% subsidy. The officer claimed that the government had achieved about 40% to 60% success in these schemes. This might well be true but my fieldwork revealed that the people living in the far-flung villages are not able to avail any of these schemes substantially. The people here mainly subsist on the output of one crop a year and many families have to depend upon the resources in the forests for survival during the winter months. As a sizable population in these pockets remains uneducated, they cannot even exploit the benefits of schemes aimed at educated unemployed youth. People participate in the parliamentary elections. But with mainstream 'development', mainstream practices of corruption and bribery have also become commonplace in the state. On a number of occasions, I noticed that even among young people corruption was taken as a part of life and not an aberration. People openly joked about getting into government service and exploiting their power for personal gains. Once I was introduced to a boy of about 5 years of age and told "he is the unfortunate son of the only engineer in the district who is not corrupt." As discussed throughout this report, the policy of granting reservation to Scheduled Tribe has not resulted in a change in the internal hierarchy of the people as such schemes are mainly being exploited by the privileged class. For the Sherthukpens who are yet to draw upon the development initiatives and who remain on the fringes of the 'new world' and its economy, living between the two worlds can be like walking a tightrope. Blissful ignorance of the 'other' has been swapped for a disturbing awareness of the mainstream and its pleasures. The awareness that beyond the high mountains and forested paths that connect their hamlets to roads which link them to cities, people lead a life different from their own—a life with schools, hospitals, electricity, government jobs and security. Hence, the development initiatives, to an extent, have resulted in the deepening of the existing hierarchies and, furthermore, have led to the emergence of a whole new set of problems and conflicts which may not be quite as straightforward to resolve.

NOTES AND REFERENCES

1. The term Nehru-Elwin Policy refers to the rapid expansion of administration under the former revivalist-protectionist approach. The policy endeavoured to achieve changes amidst least intervention in the socio-political autonomy, tribal traditions, arts and a protectionist-welfare approach towards economic development of the tribes of Arunachal Pradesh. The framework of the policy was originally framed by the Bordoloi Committee. The committee formulated the policy for the Partially Excluded Areas under undivided Assam, mainly formulated on the basis of the Report of the North-East Frontier (Assam) Tribal and Excluded Areas Sub-Committee headed by G.N. Bordoloi.
2. See Music and Dance.

Appendix

The draft of the 5th TVC or Thukpen Village Council has been furnished in this addendum and has been replicated exactly in the form available in print from the TVC. No editing or changes have been made in the main text (available as under). Additional comments have been only added in the footnotes. The purpose is to represent in its exact form an integral aspect of Sherthukpen administration and culture.

THE 5TH CHHATPU NSEY 2002

The 5th Chhatup Nsey 2002 started on 9th December 2002 at Rupa Gompa under the Chairmanship of Shri Dorji Thongdok, Head Gaon Bura, Tukpen Village Council (TVC).

The meeting started with traditional ritual performance by Khikzizi and introduction and welcome address by the Head GB,[1] Shri Dorje Thongdok.

The meeting ended on 13th December 2002 with Blu Hatohn.[2] In the meeting, a total of 33 (thirty-three) cases were taken up out of which 31 (thirty-one) cases were solved and 2 (two) cases were deferred.

Besides the cases, some amendments were made in the TVC system and Sections.

The following Sections have been framed under the Tukpen Customary Laws.

1. TVC Sections of Customary Laws

(a) Section 10: (Clause (a) Mih-mat Ru[3]) / Clause (b) Mih-mat toh-khan[4]): Rs. 10,000/- only, which is equivalent to a plot of land. The following offences shall be penalised under this section:
   - (i) Divorce of Mih-mat.
   - (ii) Attempt to murder or murder
   - (iii) Rape
   - (iv) Defaulter of Kaching

(b) Section 9 (Oboh-usu Sontong[5]): Rs. 5,000/- only. The following offences shall be penalised under this section:
   - (i) Violation of customary law
   - (ii) Act of lawlessness.
   - (iii) Land encroachment.
   - (iv) Defaulter of Chhampo[6]/Khik-zizi.

(c) Section 8(a) (Lungpu Chik-khrim[7]): Rs. 1,500/- only, which is equivalent to an ox. The fine is payable to TVC for:
   - (i) All criminal cases.
   - (ii) Violation of Duchhin.
   - (iii) Indulgence in banned activities.

(d) Section 8(b): Rs. 500/- only for:
   - (i) Suicide attempt or suicide.

(e) Section 8(c): Rs. 150/- only for:
   - (i) Kaching Satgo.
   - (ii) Duchhin B'hih-khan.

(f) Section 7(a) (Chhaw-mat Ru[8] / Chhaw-mat toh-khan): Rs. 5,000/- only.

(g) Section 7(b) (Yamlung Zognkhan[9]): Rs. 1,000/- only, which is equivalent to a calf.

(h) Section 5 (Lecso[10]): Rs. 1,000/- only, which is equivalent to a sheep or one endi cloth.

(i) Section 5 (Rong-gung[11]): Rs. 300/- for:
    (i) Minor offences.

(j) In the case of birth of illegitimate child, a fine of Rs. 3,000/- is imposed on the mother of the child.[12]

(k) In case of marriage to a foreigner, a fine of Rs. 3,000/- only has been fixed. However, marriage with a non-Arunachali Indian citizen will not be considered an offence but a marriage registration fee of Rs. 3,000/- only has to be remitted to the council.[13]

2. Ofences and Applicable Sections of Law

(a) Divorce: In case of divorce, the boy has to pay as per the following section to the girl:
    (i) Section 10 Clause (a) in case of Mih-mat Ru and Section 7(a) in case of Chhaw-mat Ru.
    (ii) Section 10 Clause (b) in case of Mih-mat toh-khan and Section 7(a) in case of Chhaw-mat toh-khan. However, this clause is not applicable in case:
        - The girl has not given birth to any child from him or
        - The girl refuses continuation of marriage without any genuine reason as judged by the council or
        - The girl herself refuses to accept this clause
    (iii) Section 9 (Oboh-usu Sontong)
    (iv) Section 8 (Lungpu Chik-khrim), this amount is payable to the TVC.
    (v) Section 7 (b) (Yamlung Zogn-khan).
    (vi) Section 5 (Lecso).

(b) Exception to the Divorce law:
    (i) if the girl has her first child born of a man other than her husband, that man will have to pay the Ru (Gum-zangmu), which includes all the sections applicable in case of divorce, except section 8(a) which will be jointly paid by the husband and wife to the TVC.

(b) Illicit relation: In case the illicit relation is proved by the council, both the girl and the boy will be fined a Chik-khrim of Rs. 1,500/- only each. However, the boy will be fined an additional amount of Rs. 5,000/- only under section 9 (Oboh-usu Sontong) to TVC.[14]

3. Death Rituals

(a) A modification to the 14th day and 21st day death rituals have been made such that the family of the deceased may NOT perform these rituals outside their village, and furthermore, the ritual will only consist of lighting Chhoeme[15] in nearby holy places. This modification has been made in view of the heavy expenditures incurred by the family of the deceased.
(b) It has been unanimously agreed upon by the TVC to ban Braiso, which means the last meal with the deceased. It is the duty of the family of the deceased to refrain from preparing food for this purpose.

4. Chhampo and Khik-zizi

(a) Defaulters of Chhampo and Khik-zizi will be penalised under Section 9 and Section 8 of the TVC Customary Laws.

5. Appeal from Jigaon

The public of Jigaon and Musaksing villages requested the TVC to exempt them from the following:

(a) Chhokok[16] tep-khan during *Wang*.[17]
(b) Yokmu-kho Sat-khan.[18]
(c) Blu-blaat.

They also proposed to perform *Chhokor* and *Wang* at Jigaon on their own.

After a prolonged discussion, the council has given the following decision.

(a) If any village wishes to perform *Chhokor* / *Wang* in their village, the council cannot prevent them from doing so.

However, the age-old system of contribution to TVC by each household in the form of Chhokok-khomi tep-khan, Yokmu-kho, Kho-satkhan, etc. cannot be exempted.[19]

(b) At the most certain, Blu-blaat can be exempted to certain villages if at all they are not able to attend the TVC Blu-blaat due to their own village Blu-blaat.

6. ST Certificate and Use of Sherthukpen Surname by a Non-shertukpen

It has been observed that many non-Sherthukpen persons are using surnames (Rung) like Thongdok, Khrimey, etc. Many of them have even procured ST Certificates. The Council has decided to complain in writing to the police regarding such non-tribal persons possessing fake ST Certificate of Sherthukpen Tribe, and request the police to seize the certificate from such a person.[20]

7. Yak Brokpus[21]

The following Brokpus will give 4 (four) Yaks every three years as Charin to the TVC, under the following four groups:

(a) Group I: Nima Tsering, Phurpa and Tamring from Changlingling Brok.
(b) Group II: Phurpa Wangdi and Naku from Didang Brok.
(c) Group III: Chhene from Khochho-khruk Brok.
(d) Group IV: Phunchu Gombu, T.Norbu and Tenzing from Broklu and Menchho Patong Brok.

8. Ban of Hunting Dogs

a) Hunting in Tukpen Council area with the help hunting dogs has been banned.[22]

9. Appointment of New Khomis[23]

(a) It has been decided to appoint the new Khomis during every Chhatpu-Nsey which shall be held every three years. This year, the following Khomis were appointed:

(i) Shri Wangchu Megegi, S/o Shri Chumbi Megeji of Thongre.

(ii) Shri Rincl Wangdi Megeji, S/o late Khandong Megeji of Rupa.

(iii) Geshe Karma, S/o Phurpa Karma of Rupa. bvc

(iv) Chheng Karma, S/o Chhono Dorke Karma of Rupa.

(v) Tashi Phuntso Thongdok, S/o late Wangdi Thongdok of Rupa.

(vi) Wangdi Sinchaji, S/o Tsering Norbu Sinchaji of Rupa.

(vii) Chumbe Sinchaji, S/o Gendan Tsering Sinchaji of Rupa.

(viii) Lam Norbu Khrimey, S/o Pema Khandu Sinchaji of Thongrey.

(ix) Lobsang Megeji, S/o Kehang Norbu Mijiji of Dikshi.

(x) Dorjee Khandu Sinchaji, S/o Phunchu Sinchaji Lingbaktang.

(xi) Pema Khandu Thongon, S/o Sang Norbu Thongon of Lingbaktang.

(xii) Phurpa Tsering Sinchaji, S/o Dorjee Norbu Sinchaji of Musaksing.

(xiii) Rinchin Phuntso Tongchi, S/o Wangchu Thongchi of Jigaon.

(xiv) Pema Dorjee Megeji, S/o Rinchin Megeji of Mukhuthing.

(xv) Pema Dorjee Dinglah, S/o Khandu Dinglah of Gorbaw.

(xvi) Pema Dorjee Dinglah, S/o Chewang Dinglah of Gorbaw.

(xvii) Sang Tesring Dinglah, S/o Khandu Dinglah of Gorbaw.

(xviii) Dorjee Chewang Dinglah, S/o Leki Khandu Dinglah of Jigaon.

(xix) Rinchin Wangdi Thongdok, S/o Netan Dorjee Thongdok of Jigaon.

(xx) Gombu Mosobi, S/o Dorjee Chewang Mosobi of Jigaon.

(xxi) Tensing Dinglah, S/o Tsering Chewang Dinglah of Jigaon.

(xxii) Nawang Norbu Dinglah, S/o Nima Dorjee Dinglah of Jigaon.

(xxiii) Shri Lam Norbu Khrimey, S/o late Pema Khandu Sinchaji of Thongrey.

(xxiv) Shri Lobsang Megeji, S/o Shri Kejang Norbu Mijiji of Dikshi.

(xxv) Shri Dorjee Khandu Sinchaji, S/o Shri Phunchu Sinchaji of Lingbaktang.

(xxvi) Shri Pema Kandu Thongon, S/o Shri Sang Norbu Thongon of Lingbaktang.

(xxvii) Shri Phurpa Tsering Sinchaji, S/o Shri Dorjee Norbu Sinchaji of Musaksing.

(xxviii) Shri Rinchin Phuntso Thongchi, S/o Shri Wangchu Thongchi of Jigaon.

(xxix) Shri Pema Dorjee Dinglah, S/o Shri Rinchin Megeji of Mukhuthing.

(xxx) Shri Pema Dorjee Dinglah, S/o Shri Chewang Dinglah of Gorbaw.

(xxxi) Shri Sang Tsering Dinglah, S/o Shri Khandu Dinglah of Gorbaw.

(xxxii) Shri Nima Dorjee Khrimey, S/o Shri Wangdi Khrimey of Gorbaw.

(xxxiii) Shri Dorjee Chewang Dinglah, S/o Shri Leki Khandu Dinglah of Jigaon.

(xxxiv) Shri Rinchin Wangdi Thongdok, S/o Shri Netan Dorjee Thongdok of Jigaon.

(xxxv) Shri Gombu Mosobi, S/o Shri Tsering Chewang Dinglah of Jigaon.

(xxxvi) Shri Nawang Norbu Dinglah, S/o Shri Nima Dorjee Dinglah of Jigaon.

(xxxvii) Shri Tsering Dorjee Sinchaji, S/o Shri Pema Khandu Sinchaji of Jigaon.

(xxxviii) Shri Topgey Dinglah, S/o Shri Ledo Dinglah of Membachur.

(xxxix) Shri Chhetan Bijiji, S/o Shri Sang Tsering Bijiji of Membachur.

10. DRAFTING COMMITTEE MEMBERS

(a)	Shri Prem Dorjee Wangja	: Chairman
(b)	Shri D. K. Thongon	: Member
(c)	Shri Topgyal Thongdok	: "
(d)	Shri D.P. Thongdok	: "
(e)	Shri N.D. Thongdok	: "
(f)	Shri P.T. Thongon	: "
(g)	Shri S.C. Wangja	: "

CONCLUSION

The meeting concluded with speech by the Head GB, Shri Dorji Thongdok in the Blu Hatohn.

(P.D. Wangja)	(Dorji Thongdok)
Chairman, Drafting Committee	Head GB, TVC Rupa

NOTES AND REFERENCES

1. *Gaonburah.*
2. Council picnic attended by men only.
3. Thong lady. *Ru* – It is customary for a man to give something to his brother-in-law after his wife's death.
4. Returning the woman; only in case of divorce.
5. GB's fine. This money is given to the GBs. They are free to either give the money to the council or keep it with themselves.
6. Sherthukpen dance troupe or 'dance party'.
7. Misconduct or any crime deemed as such by the council.
8. Chao woman.
9. Household humiliation clearance.
10. Forgiveness.
11. Begging the council's forgiveness.

12. The rationale for not fining the man: Unless the woman is punished, the name of the father will not be revealed and the child might have to be 'illegitimate' throughout his life. It must be mentioned that there is a strong social taboo in the Sherthukpen society against illegitimate children.
13. In the context of 'marriage to a foreigner', the social approval depends upon the place where the foreigner originates from. Marriage with Nepalese, Bhutanese and Tibetans is frowned upon because the Nepalese population in the state mainly comprises migrant labourers; the Bhutanese have traditionally been migrants in the area who were granted refuge and thus the Sherthukpens view them as socially subordinate; and the Tibetans in the area are mainly refugees and thus landless people. Much like the other people who largely live off the land, the Sherthukpens are deeply attached to their land and consider marriage in a landless family as an unworthy proposition. This is so regardless of the fact that the Tibetans are otherwise considered a culturally refined race. Curiously, I was told that per chance if a Sherthukpen were to marry, say, a European or an American, the same superciliousness would not be imposed.
14. The man is charged with an additional amount because the TVC considers it an indirect insult as he is guilty of a crime he should have already confessed to.
15. Holy lamp.
16. The Thukpen Council is divided into seven *chhokoks* or blocks. Each block is assigned with different duties which are rotated.
17. *Wang* is a Lamaist festival.
18. It is the collection of tax by the GBs and members from the various blocks. This tax is paid in clothes which are later returned. This is observed as a formality as with the coming of the monetary economy and better communication, such exchange has become redundant today. However, the custom continues to be observed simply for the sake of continuing a tradition that would otherwise die out.
19. The tax paid by each household is as follows: about 50 kg of maize, 1 kg chilies, 20 to 30 litres of *lopani* and cash (RS. 50 to 500).
20. This is mainly pertaining to the children of non-Sherthukpens married to Sherthukpen women.

21. The people who rear yaks also have to pay a tax.
22. Hunting with the help of dogs has been banned because hunting in this manner amounts to poaching as the game is caught in very large numbers. Hence, it has been banned.
23. Households.

Glossary

Acchi	Father
Anno	Elder sister
Ara	Brother
Arah	Intoxicating drink
Bakhi	Bamboo platform hung over the hearth to store perishable food
Betang	Tibetan silver coin
Blang	Dormitory
Blu Hatohn	Council picnic attended by men only
Blu-blaat	Collective work group
Bogre	Locally woven knapsack
Bokpi	Dish made by boiling finger-millet flour
Brampu	Labour group sought for agricultural or construction works
Busties	Hamlets
Cher	Round cane vessel used for oil extraction
Chhampo	Sherthukpen dance troupe
Chhatpu Nsey	Thukpen Village Council
Chhaw-mat	Chao woman
Chhlo	Father's elder brother

Chhoeme	Holy lamp
Chhokar	Lamaist festival celebrated in the fourth month of the lunar calendar
Chhokok	Blocks into which the Thukpen Council is divided
Chok	Blessed food
Chomo	Dish made by stir-frying millet flour and chopped onions
Chorten	Stone structure that houses relics of a dead person
Churpi	Cheese made of milk or soyabeans
Dao	Local knife
Daun	Bag woven from cotton thread
Dongzurs	Stone shrine
Dukang	Dark cell for jailing miscreants
Dung Rhongmu	Wooden phallus symbol
Dzizi	Local priest
Endi	Assam silk
Gaonburah	Headman of the village
Gompa	Monastery
Grima ku	Red dye obtained from the Monpas
Gurdam	Cap made of Yak hair
Haa	Food
Haats	Foothill bazaars
Hun	Traditional Sherthukpen songs
In-e-bu	Female Lama
Jabrang	Local herb used in cooking
Jhum	Slash and burn cultivation
Jomotho	Local mustard
Jooyooum bu	Co-operative group for internal security
Jumu	Millet flour
Jung	Village Council
Jungme	Meeting Elders
Kaching Pa	Voluntary guards
Kachinpo	Servant
Khengpo	Traditional dances
Khik	Powerful Lo diety

Khiksaba — Important Sherthukpen festival celebrated in Rupa

Khomi — Household

Khrangpu — Traditional Sherthukpen food

Kros — Holy caves

Lesco — Forgiveness

Luduk — Full sleeves jacket

Lungpu Chik-khrim — Misconduct or any crime deemed as such by the council

Machaan — Platform made on a tree to facilitate hunting

Maney — Stone wall placed with tablets that read *Om mani padme hum*

Mih-mat — Thong lady

Mithun — Bos frontalis

Mukhaks — Colourful handloom belt

Orang — Flute

Orang — Hand-held musical instruments

Pam — Village

Pechha — Historical treatises

Phak — Local beer

Phak/Lopani — Local beer

Photenya — Harvest ceremony

Phu-lapsang — Ceremony performed to summon rain

Pita — Fried noodles

Pooja — Prayer ceremony

Prasaad — Blessed food

Ru — Price that a man has to give to his brother-in-law after his wife's death

Sapo Bla — Common hunting group

Sinkhoo — Sleeveless long gown

Tashi topa — House warming feast

Tepa — Help or assistance

Thok — Cane bag used in preparation of *Phak*

Thongs — High caste Sherthukpens

Thuik — Village

Thukpen — Village of the Thongs

Tonga	Coarse Bhutanese woollen cloth
Tormas	Figures of flour made during ceremonies
Wang	Two-day festival celebrated to pay homage to Lord Buddha
Yams	Houses
Yanlaks	Bhutanese immigrants
Yanpo blu	Common fishing party

Select Bibliography

Balagangadhara, S.N. 1994. *The Heathen in His Blindness*. Leiden: Brill.

Census of India. 1971. *Socio-Economic Survey of Rupa*, Series-1 India, Part VI C. New Delhi: Ministry of Home Affairs.

Chattopadhyay, T. 1990. *Lepchas and their Heritage*. Delhi: BR Publishers.

Chowdhury, J.N. 1973. *Arunachal Panorama*. Shillong: J. Chowdhury.

Das, Gurudas. 1995. *Tribes of Arunachal Pradesh in Transition*. New Delhi: Vikas.

Dunbar, G.D.S. 1915. *The Abors and Gallongs*, Vol. V of ASB. Calcutta.

Elwin, Verrier. 1958. *Myths of the North-East Frontier of India*. Shillong: North-East Frontier Agency.

——. 1959. *The Art of the North-East Frontier of India*. Shillong: North-East Frontier Agency.

——. 1988. *Democracy in NEFA*. Itanagar: Directorate of Research, Government of Arunachal Pradesh.

Fürer-Haimendorf, Christoph von. 1982. *Highlanders of Arunachal Pradesh: Anthropological Research in North-East India*. New Delhi: Vikas.

Gowloog, R.R. 1995. *Lingthem Revisited. Social Change in a Lepcha Village of North Sikkim*. New Delhi: Har Anand.

Grewal, Dalvinder Singh (Col.). 1997. *Tribes of Arunachal Pradesh: Identity, Culture and Language*, Vol. I. Delhi: South Asian.

Nair, P. Thankappan. 1985. *Tribes of Arunachal Pradesh*. Guwahati: Spectrum.

Panchani, Chander Sheikhar. 1989. *Arunachal Pradesh: Religion, Culture and Society*.

Sarkar, Niranjan. 1980. *Buddhism among the Monpas and Sherdukpens*. Itanagar: Directorate of Research, Government of Arunachal Pradesh.

Sharma, R.R.P. 1961. *The Sherdukpens*. Shillong: Research Department, NEFA Secretariat.

Index